AF182576

PARDON OUR FRENCH

life

PARDON OUR FRENCH

The Parisian Way to a Happier Life

ALEX DURAND and TOM CARLES

with Allie Kingsley Baker

PENGUIN LIFE

VIKING
An imprint of Penguin Random House LLC
1745 Broadway, New York, NY 10019
penguinrandomhouse.com

Copyright © 2026 by Alex Durand and Tom Carles

Penguin Random House values and supports copyright. Copyright fuels creativity, encourages diverse voices, promotes free speech, and creates a vibrant culture. Thank you for buying an authorized edition of this book and for complying with copyright laws by not reproducing, scanning, or distributing any part of it in any form without permission. You are supporting writers and allowing Penguin Random House to continue to publish books for every reader. Please note that no part of this book may be used or reproduced in any manner for the purpose of training artificial intelligence technologies or systems.

A Penguin Life Book

VIKING is a registered trademark of Penguin Random House LLC.

DESIGNED BY AMANDA DEWEY

LIBRARY OF CONGRESS CONTROL NUMBER PERMALINK:
https://lccn.loc.gov/2026000404

ISBN 9780593994764 (hardcover)
ISBN 9780593994771 (ebook)

Printed in the United States of America
1st Printing

The authorized representative in the EU for product safety and compliance is Penguin Random House Ireland, Morrison Chambers, 32 Nassau Street, Dublin D02 YH68, Ireland, https://eu-contact.penguin.ie.

For the francophiles, this one's for you.

Merci pour tout.

(Thank you for everything.)

CONTENTS

Introduction: BIENVENUE TO OUR WORLD *ix*

Chapter 1. OUR STORY: TWO FRENCHIES LOST IN AMERICA *1*

Part I. THE FRENCH MINDSET

Chapter 2. CHOOSE CURIOSITY EVERY DAY *31*

Chapter 3. PROTECT YOUR PRIVATE LIFE *51*

Chapter 4. REDEFINE THE HUSTLE *58*

Part II. LIVING À LA FRANÇAISE

Chapter 5. LOVE BOLDLY *77*

Chapter 6. SAVOR EVERY BITE *101*

Chapter 7. KEEP STYLE SIMPLE *130*

Chapter 8. BUILD FRIENDSHIPS THAT LAST *157*

Part III. THE FRENCH ART OF APPRECIATING LIFE

Chapter 9. TREAT THE EARTH LIKE A FRIEND *181*

Chapter 10. SEE ART EVERYWHERE *198*

Chapter 11. FIND JOY IN RITUAL *213*

In Conclusion: MAKE EVERY DAY MORE FRENCH *231*

Acknowledgments 235

Glossary of French Terms 237

INTRODUCTION: Bienvenue to Our World

A few years ago, we were just two kids from Paris, fresh off the plane and taking our first steps in our new home for the next four years: the United States. Barely able to string a sentence together in English, we were now chasing our soccer dreams in colleges across the Atlantic. We didn't know much beyond the French way of living, but we were up for the adventure. That's how we ended up in places like Nowhere, Ohio, and Smalltown, Mississippi—far from the bustling American cities that graced our TV screens growing up.

Despite the initial shock, we'd end up falling madly in love with American culture. The U.S. welcomed us with open arms, big dreams, and even bigger breakfasts. We loved the displays of patriotism, the pervasive sense of individualism, and the "anyone can do anything" vibe. Even now, we still call the States home.

What we didn't expect is that we'd come to appreciate the little (and major) things that made us French, in a way we never had before. In France, we never questioned our flexible schedules, our focus on staying present, or our willingness to engage in strong debate. It was just life. But in America, where hustle is king and time is sliced into efficient little blocks, we started to notice the contrast. We saw how the French way of slowing down, making space for pleasure, and valuing real connection could bring something worthwhile and refreshing to how we lived, loved, dressed, dined, worked, and communicated in our every day.

This mix of cultures sparked something in us. In fact, we fell so in love with that contrast that we started sharing our perspective online in short, fun videos about the French language and lifestyle. Somehow, that turned into millions of views, a community of over two million, and some incredible opportunities, like attending the White House Correspondents' Dinner and covering the 2024 Summer Olympics in our hometown of Paris. It turned out, more people were hungry for the French way of life than we'd thought.

We're Alex and Tom, aka AT Frenchies. We weren't trying to become cultural ambassadors or go viral online. Honestly, we just wanted to try something different—a fun life experience, a shot at playing pro soccer in the States, and a chance to see what life had in store for us. Turns out, it had a few surprises: a couple of brutal injuries, a global pandemic, and a whole lot of unexpected lessons. Now we're here—not on the pitch playing soccer, but on your bookshelf, sharing a love letter to the French way of life and why it's worth stealing a few ideas from.

This book isn't about berets, baguettes, or the cliché of a grumpy Parisian waiter. It's about the soul of French culture—the *art de vivre*, the savoring of life's pleasures, the stubborn refusal to rush a good meal or a great conversation. It's about staying curious like a kid, loving fiercely without losing yourself, and building friendships that feel like family.

We're not here to lecture or sell you a lifestyle seminar. We're just sharing what we've lived—from the cobblestone streets of Paris to the winding highways of the States—because we believe the French way can light a spark in anyone, anywhere.

This book is our way of passing that torch to you. It's about grabbing the French mindset and making it work wherever you are—without moving to France or mastering a perfect accent (though we can help with that). Want to slow down and actually taste your food? We've got tips for that. Need to build a crew that's more ride-or-die than Wi-Fi? We'll show you how. Curious about keeping your spark alive, no matter your age? That's in here, too. From savoring a single perfect crêpe to dodging burnout with a well-timed nap, we're spilling the secrets that keep the French sharp, sane, and maybe just a bit smug.

We're not promising a magic fix—life's too messy for that. But what we are offering is a playbook, tested through our own stumbles and triumphs, to help you live with a little more zest, a little less stress, and a whole lot of French flair.

So, flip the page. Push your to-do list aside, crack open a bottle of whatever's handy, and dive into a world where life's not a race—it's a promenade.

Bienvenue, mes amis. (Welcome, my friends.) Let's make it a good one.

PARDON OUR FRENCH

Chapter 1.

OUR STORY: TWO FRENCHIES LOST IN AMERICA

Before we get into it, we want to share our journey of what brought us to the U.S. in the first place. As in the rest of the book, you'll hear from each of us individually—we'll let you know who's doing the talking—and from both of us together.

ALEX'S STORY

Good news usually comes with a phone call. Bad news? It tends to arrive in an envelope.

I was now clutching one of those envelopes, walking beside my dad toward his car in a hospital parking lot in Burgundy. He'd driven four hours from Paris for this moment, ready to face the possibility that my childhood dream—becoming a professional soccer player—might just be over.

I was fifteen years old, a year into my time at the Dijon Football Côte d'Or academy, a youth pipeline for one of France's top professional soccer clubs. Picture a middle schooler getting drafted to the Yankees' minor leagues while earning a full scholarship to a prestigious boarding school—that's how big a deal it was. The year before, the pros had told me, "Forget your friends, forget fast food, forget living at home. If you want to go pro, this is your shot." That was all I'd needed to hear to apply.

Some might say fourteen is too young to make life-altering decisions, but in France, this responsibility is thrust onto you much earlier. Where we generally value a slow pace in the micro—think long, languid dinners and meandering walks along the Seine—in the macro, everything happens sooner. American teens can wait until college to figure out their futures, but we pick our paths—medicine, law, soccer, you name it—by fourteen. Few, if any, adults migrate out of that track once on it. This is the French way.

For me, the decision was simple. I was good enough to get noticed as a goalkeeper, and I wanted to play professionally. So, sign me up. I left home, moved four hours away, and joined a ruthless four-year feeder program. If you were good enough, you stayed until you turned eighteen. If you were exceptional, you had a shot at the pro team—and by *exceptional*, I mean you needed to be one of the top two players in your class.

My first year was a total wake-up call. For me, soccer had always been about teamwork and shared victories. At the academy, it was every guy for himself. Nobody was looking out for each other, and every tackle felt like a fight for survival.

Adding to the pressure, I was a goalkeeper. Goalkeepers are usually expected to be at least six foot two. I wasn't. I was undersized for the position. I'd been drinking milk religiously since I was five, at the urging of my father, who was small himself. He was sure if I just consumed enough, I would grow beyond my genes. The growth spurt never happened.

In France, they do MRI scans of your wrist to look at the bones, mostly to determine your true age. But they also do it to determine how tall you might grow. So at sixteen, at the end of my first year, they asked me to take the test.

When my dad got wind of that, he freaked out. If the results showed I'd stay on the shorter side, my dream—what my dad and I had been working on for a decade, my entire childhood—would be over.

Which brings us back to the envelope. It contained the results of that MRI. I sat in the car, staring at it, holding my breath. My dad was there, silent beside me. I knew what the paper would say, but a flicker of hope still held on. I tore it open and read the words confirming what I feared: My growth plates were nearly done. Five foot ten. Not enough to make the pros.

I cried like crazy, more than I'd care to admit. Everything I'd worked for, gone in a single medical report. I was being removed from the academy in year two based on a prediction for how big I would be by year four. I headed back home to Paris, feeling as if my world had just collapsed. In many ways, it genuinely had.

So at sixteen, in true teenage fashion, I partied to deal with my despair. In France, you can get away with drinking at that age, and I took full advantage. Nightclubs, late nights—I wasn't spiraling out of control, but I was definitely living it up, drifting from one day to the next. I still played soccer, but only because I was good at it, not because I thought it was my future.

Actually, I had no aim for my future. I had no clue what else I was good at or even capable of being except for a soccer player.

But somewhere amid the fog, a spark began to ignite. I realized I needed a chance to break free—a shot at a new beginning in a place where I still had plenty of runway to a professional soccer career and, if nothing else, a bit more time to figure out what—if anything—I could pursue professionally.

Little did I know that opportunity would be connected to my childhood friend, Tom Carles. Another soccer player on a wildly similar path that would soon cross with mine.

TOM'S STORY

It's wild how one moment can flip your life upside down—not because it's massive on its own, but because it kick-starts a chain of events that completely changes the trajectory of your future.

Growing up, like Alex, soccer wasn't just my passion; it was my entire world. From the time I could walk, anything that even vaguely resembled a ball, I kicked. At school, in the street, at home—if it was round, I sent it flying. Year after year, I did nothing but obsess over soccer. When I wasn't playing, I was watching. When I wasn't watching, I was playing the latest soccer video game. Every kick, every goal, every drop of sweat—it was all in pursuit of growing up to sign a contract to play soccer for a professional club.

To me, this was as righteous a quest as any to dedicate my life to. But at school, my obsession with soccer wasn't seen as ambition—it was seen as defiance. My school was strict. Whisper in class? Two-hour Sunday detention. Look out the window for too long? Another detention. Prioritize anything over coursework? You were a lost cause. My teachers saw my passion as rebellion, my determination as disrespect. To them, I was a troublemaker. Sure, sometimes I was guilty. And when I was, I owned up to it. But there were plenty of times when I wasn't, and they still punished me. It didn't matter what was true—what mattered was that I wasn't the quiet, obedient student they wanted me to be.

One of the many things I would later learn to love about American culture is that they celebrate passion and individualism beyond conformity and obedience, even in the classroom. It's a part of the culture I celebrate most.

Thankfully, my parents embody this spirit. They raised me to be independent. They didn't criticize my focus or determination or goals on the field, and they didn't push me in that direction either. My parents weren't ones to hover over my practices or games. They came sometimes, but they knew I preferred to figure things out for myself. Advice was never forced upon me—until one game, when my dad attended. His advice should have been the one thing I listened to.

I'd been asked to participate in a tournament where, if I performed well, I could earn a spot in the Nantes academy; like Dijon, it was one of the most prestigious youth academies in France. It was a tryout, an opportunity to prove myself in front of scouts and coaches from one of the country's top academies. The stakes couldn't have been higher. I was butting up against my sixteenth birthday. Once you pass that threshold in France, you are no longer as desirable for a professional youth academy. You can still become a pro soccer player, but the odds drop dramatically if you do not get one of these coveted spots.

Before the big tournament, I had one last match to play for the Athletic Club de Boulogne-Billancourt (ACBB) in

Paris, where I played. My dad pulled me aside at halftime and suggested I sit out the rest of the game to save my legs for the tournament and avoid injury. I shrugged it off. I'd never been injured before. I played every minute, always. That was my attitude. You don't play soccer to play thirty minutes or forty-five. You play ninety minutes. That's the length of the game, and you play it to win.

Then, as if my father had jinxed me—or maybe it was my own hubris—in the second half, I took a brutal tackle the likes of which I'd never felt before. An older, stronger player hit me hard, just above the knee. I went down, a sharp pain shooting through my quad. It ended my day, but I thought it was just a bruise. Nothing I couldn't shake off.

A week later, I arrived for the week of practice in Nantes ahead of the tournament. For the first three days, I was fine. While my knee started to get uncomfortable, I was able to play through and acquit myself well. However, when I woke up on day four, my knee had swelled to the size of a watermelon. I could barely walk, let alone play.

Then came the medical room and the confirmation by MRI: windshield wiper syndrome. I needed four months to recover. Four months might as well have been four years. My last shot at an academy was just that—a shot. And I had missed it.

The Nantes coach came to see me. He told me how sorry he was. That he had been excited to work with me. That I had something special. "It's a shame," he said. He was trying to comfort me, but it was only making me feel worse. He was all but confirming that my dream was over. I had never felt more lost in my life than I did listening to him talk.

Then the academy director called me in. I expected some exit paperwork and a formal goodbye. Instead, he gave me a lifeline.

"We work with an agency that connects players like you with universities in the United States," he said. "They help with scholarships. Are you interested?"

Without hesitation, I said, "Yes."

I didn't know much about soccer in the U.S., but I knew I wasn't ready to quit. If France wasn't the place, I'd find another way.

That night, I went to bed as a French kid. The next morning, I woke up with a new goal: to become an American soccer player. The agency guided me through the process, and while it was hard leaving behind everything I knew, I had something I hadn't felt since my injury: hope.

It was a hope I would eventually get to share with Alex.

MEETING AMERICA (by Tom)

Alex and I met on a soccer field when we were twelve, spending pretty much every day after school running drills until our legs gave out, turning competitive drive into friendship. By the time we turned fifteen, we'd lost contact with each other while we chased our individual paths to pro soccer (you know how that turned out). When Alex came back from Dijon feeling pretty lost, we linked up again and I brought him into my friend group. We were all high-level student athletes who understood the pain of falling out of a major career opportunity. Something about that shared drive and disappointment brought us close together again, fast.

But I couldn't shake my newfound goal: to become an American soccer player. While Alex and the others enjoyed their newfound freedom in the Paris nightclubs, I remained focused on securing a spot on an American college soccer team.

It didn't take long to bring Alex on board. As graduation grew ever closer, Alex realized his path forward was narrowing more rapidly than he wished. Maybe this idea of American college could be a viable option for him, too. America could be our fresh start, our promised land. In France, life moves with ruthless efficiency. At sixteen, you're expected to lock into a career trajectory with little room for deviation. We weren't ready for such finality. Soccer was our passion, and we weren't prepared to surrender our dreams or prematurely dive into a corporate career when we could use our talent to expand our options overseas.

The American education system is much different. You can declare a major late. You can even have dual majors. You can play collegiate soccer with a chance to go pro years after that window would be closed to you in France. It was a long shot, and we didn't know much about America—but the one thing we did know was that the U.S. loves an underdog story. So, Alex and I made it our mission to do everything required of us to be able to go to college in the United States.

First step, polish up our English. Our English was rough back then. Actually, "rough" is being generous. We spent long nights hunched over textbooks, trying to wrap our heads around why *read* and *lead* rhyme in one sentence, and *read* and *red* rhyme in the next. It felt like every grammar rule came with a footnote that said, "Just kidding—not always!" The SAT study guides became our bedtime stories, and Google Translate was basically our night nurse.

Next up: Pitch ourselves to colleges. Looking back, the number of emails we sent is almost embarrassing. We'd film highlight reels of ourselves playing soccer, edit them to make ourselves look like the next big thing, then write these painfully formal emails in what we thought was proper English. The silence we got back was deafening. Months on end of throwing coins into a bottomless well, with not a ripple of validation in return.

We were starting to lose faith in our efforts when Alex's papa, Bruno, who'd always been his champion in this quest, discovered a highly touted Adidas soccer camp in Philadelphia. Picture the most stereotypical French father—serious, practical, zero patience for nonsense—suddenly becoming our unlikely rescuer. He signed up Alex for the camp and agreed to take me along, too. He thought this would be a good opportunity to get us seen by people stateside.

Just like that, we were heading to America. First stop: Manhattan.

New York City hit us like a truck. Everything was massive—the buildings, the food portions, the personalities. We probably looked ridiculous, taking photos of literally everything. Regular stuff to Americans was mind-blowing to us. The scale and scope of our surroundings, the energy and speed of cars and pedestrians, and the energy of the city overwhelmed us in every way. I still have a photo of my first New York breakfast like it's some kind of historical artifact: fried chicken, waffles, syrup, plus a side of toast—all on one plate? Who eats fried chicken for breakfast? This mass quantity alone was both comically absurd and a revelation. Why doesn't *everyone* eat fried chicken for breakfast?!

And the fashion! If you could call it that? So many people were wearing sweatpants and casual clothes. Were they going shopping, or were they going to bed? We felt greatly overdressed. In Paris, you don't go out in the same clothes you went to bed in the previous night. People are more pulled together, even when running errands or simply leaving the house. You would never see a Parisian woman running to the supermarket in sweatpants, a hoodie, and UGG slippers. This widely accepted style fascinated us, as did the incredible access to brand-name fashion.

The Supreme store incident still makes me laugh. Alex, who'd grown up wearing nothing but minimalist fashion, label-less shirts free from in-your-face brand names, on par with French culture, suddenly—overtaken by the energy of NYC maybe—decided he absolutely had to have a classic block-logo Supreme T-shirt. He'd never be able to get his hands on such a rare thing at home.

We get to the Supreme store, and the line is wrapped around the block. Bruno, Alex's dad, took one look and just said, "Non." He was not about to wait two hours to buy an overpriced T-shirt with a gaudy logo on it. "You're not a billboard, Alex," I remember him saying. What followed was an incredible father-son showdown in rapid-fire French, right there on the sidewalk in front of the whole line.

"This is the holy grail of shirts, Papa!" Alex said.

"This is shit!" his papa fired back.

"It's impossible-to-come-by-in-Paris shit!"

"Nonsense! Wasting two hours of your life can be done in Paris!"

Guess who won that argument? I think Alex still gets fired up at the thought of that shirt that got away. Just ask him about it.

When we arrived at the soccer camp in Philly a few days later, we were hit with another reality check. The American players were enormous. We showed up looking like we'd been on a strict diet of espresso and cigarettes by comparison. These giants had strength training in high school, while we thought doing push-ups in our bedrooms was a serious routine. In France you can't even legally enter a proper gym until you are sixteen. Even then, serious athletes don't start lifting until they're eighteen. These American kids were pumping iron as soon as they were pumping testosterone at eleven and twelve years old.

Size disparity aside, I made the All-Star team. Alex, despite being the best goalkeeper there, was overlooked—pun intended (sorry, Alex!). The coaches in America said he was too tiny to be a goalkeeper. Go figure. Brand new continent. Same damn issue.

I was really looking forward to playing in the All-Star game. It was an opportunity to showcase my skills against the best players there, but then it rained—just a normal thunderstorm—and they canceled it entirely. Are you kidding me? We couldn't believe it. In France, we'd play through anything short of a meteor strike. Who stops playing soccer because the field is wet and you could be struck by lightning? Ridiculous.

As fate would have it, when we went back to New York before flying home the next day, it was the Fourth of July. Standing on the hotel balcony watching the fireworks over the city, sparkling flickers of light ricocheting off the reflections of skyscrapers while Miley Cyrus's "Party in the U.S.A." blasted, Alex and I knew we had to make this move happen. The energy was incredible and like nothing we had experienced before. The unflinching patriotism and pride was intoxicating, wholly different from where we'd come from—in France, people simply don't have the same sense of national pride. We were moved by what we witnessed and wanted to be a part of it.

It wasn't just the fireworks—it was everything we'd experienced throughout our visit. In the U.S., random people want to make you feel good about your day. They are always smiling at you for no reason. They'll start a conversation out of nowhere or even compliment you without knowing who you are. This is nothing like France, where people keep to themselves and reserve conversation and smiles for those they know. It actually caught us off guard—in a good way. The result was a really positive vibe that made us feel welcomed.

Also, everything in the U.S. felt bigger. Everything! The roads, the houses, the distances, the shops, the meals. But it went beyond the physical space. There was a feeling that anything was possible, that there was literally enough space for us to do whatever we wanted—to accomplish things, to grow, to truly be ourselves.

This is not the case in France. In fact, it's so much harder to be an entrepreneur in France due to the strict labor laws and high tax rate. I think it discourages a lot of people from even trying to go at it on their own or to take a chance and start something. America just feels different in that way. As if they welcome the new. They welcome the challenge. They welcome someone who wants to do things differently or walk to the beat of their own drum.

Recently, a friend of mine asked me if I felt more American or French. I answered that France is where I feel most at home, but the U.S. is where I feel like myself. I feel like I am in the right place for who I am—and I had that feeling the very first time I set foot here.

Beyond pursuing my soccer career and going to university, this was what made me want to be part of the U.S.: the positive energy and the feeling that you can take risks, start something, and just go for it.

THE WORK PAYS OFF (by Tom)

Back in France, we doubled down. More emails, more highlight reels, more English practice. But still, nothing. It was getting really bleak. It was May of our graduating year, and we did not yet know what would come next for either of us. Until we did.

One day, completely out of nowhere, Alex gets a call from Coach Eric Reed at Malone University in Canton, Ohio. He simply says, "You're in." Alex is stunned into silence. Who? What? Coach Reed goes on.

"I love your tape and your attitude. You're without a doubt the smallest goalkeeper I've ever looked at, but I have no doubt you'll be the one making a difference on the field." Alex is elated and accepts the offer on the spot. It is a dream come true.

Meanwhile, I'm happy for Alex but stuck in limbo myself. I have some interest. Both Hawaii and Kansas make me an offer but can't give me enough money to make it work for my budget, so I am forced to decline. After that, I get radio silence.

As June rolls around, running out of options, I email Malone myself, to see if they would be interested. I also email Mississippi College, where a couple of our other friends had been accepted on a tennis scholarship. Malone never replies, but Mississippi calls back with the most underwhelming "We're interested" in history. A vague, terse interaction leaves me unsure of the real degree of their interest.

No matter. Without another word I get their acceptance letter in the mail a week later with an almost full scholarship. I don't even hesitate. I was headed to Mississippi, y'all!

We'd actually done it. Two French guys who could barely string together a sentence in English had somehow studied, talked, and kicked their way into a student visa and a fresh outlook on their futures. We didn't know much about Ohio or Mississippi, but we knew they were somewhere in America, and that we could play soccer there. That was enough.

Looking back now, the whole thing seems almost impossible. We really just packed up our lives, left everything we knew, and moved to a country where we could barely order lunch. It was the start of an incredible adventure to come—and a reminder that sometimes the best adventures start with someone telling you no.

LIVING THE DREAM . . . OR SO WE THOUGHT (by Alex)

I knew nothing about Ohio. In my mind, America meant New York City and Philadelphia—bright lights, towering skyscrapers, the chaos of yellow taxis weaving through the streets. That was the dream I had conjured up. But when I stepped off the plane in Canton, a different reality smacked me in the face: America is a very large and diverse place with people from any and all walks of life.

"Holy shit, did I take the wrong flight?" I muttered under my breath, my stomach sinking. This wasn't the America I had imagined. No skyscrapers. No bustling streets filled with energy. Instead, I found myself in what looked like the set of an old-fashioned postcard—a quiet, rural town with endless fields and an airport so small I wondered if I had landed in someone's backyard.

That initial disappointment, that gnawing fear that I had made a colossal mistake, didn't last long. The moment I stepped onto campus, everything changed. This place, this self-contained city, was nothing like what I had pictured, but in the best possible way. You could do everything here—eat, shop, date, party—all without ever leaving campus. It was a world of its own, full of life and opportunity. In France, you have none of this. There is no campus life. No sorority or frat houses, no sprawling towns associated with universities. Like in grade school, university in France is not a lifestyle. It's a place to learn and nothing more. The fear melted away, replaced by a thrill I hadn't expected.

But then came the soccer field—or rather, the lack of one. What I had dreamed of as a pristine, professional-grade pitch was really just a stretch of grass beside the highway. No stadium. No bleachers. Just a makeshift field where we hauled our own nets and trained like we were playing pickup games in a neighborhood park.

I won't lie, it was disheartening at first. But what we lacked in infrastructure, we made up for in heart. That patch of grass became our battleground, our proving ground. It was raw, but it was ours. In a way, it brought us together even more.

And then there was the team—our ragtag crew, driven by passion and a deep hunger to prove ourselves. Our first season was nothing short of legendary. We dominated. We played like our futures depended on it—because, for some of us, they did. Suddenly, I wasn't just a student. I became known as the Frenchie, embraced by others as something of a campus celebrity. For the first time since I was fourteen, I felt that deep, unbreakable bond of a team—a brotherhood that transcended language barriers and backgrounds. My English was still shaky, but none of that mattered on the field. Soccer was our common language, and it spoke louder than any words ever could.

That season reignited something inside me—hope. Real, tangible hope. Canton, Ohio, might not have been Times Square, but for me, it had become the epicenter of possibility. This wasn't the end—it was just the beginning. Maybe, just maybe, I could go pro in the U.S. For the first time in a long while, I truly believed in myself again.

Tom, on the other hand, was having a different experience in Mississippi. He didn't get a hero's welcome. The team already had plenty of international players, and Tom was just another name on the roster. Worse, he spent most of the first half of the season on the bench, watching from the sidelines, waiting for his chance.

When that chance finally came, Tom made the most of it. On his first possession, he scored. A perfect, clinical finish. And in true Tom fashion—rebellious, fearless, and utterly unapologetic—he turned to his coach, tapped his wrist, and smirked as if to say, "About time you put me in." The coach yanked him right back off the field, benching him again. Tom had always had a complicated relationship with authority.

Then came the injury. Preseason his sophomore year, Tom suffered a leg injury. Determined as he was, in his mind he'd already decided to play through the pain so he could stay on the field. However, when it was revealed by doctors to be a brutal break of the fibula, Tom knew his season was over. He committed immediately to getting back as soon as possible. With the help of a budding romance (more on her later), he did just that. He zeroed in on his rehab and attacked it with all the zeal he goes after everything with.

Off the field, Tom's experience was slightly better. His roommate, Coco, was a Peruvian guy who spoke only Spanish. Tom barely spoke English. They communicated the only way they could—by whistling. Need the remote? Whistle. Want to use the bathroom? Whistle. Need quiet? Whistle. It was absolutely not ideal, but they made it work and became great friends.

What did excite us both, though, was our first American spring break. My God, what an experience that was. We decided to meet up in Panama City for a week of pure chaos. Tom brought Coco, along with François and Shane—our friends from France who had gone to Mississippi to play tennis. I packed up my French friend Simon, along with some other fellows we'd befriended, and off we went.

If you haven't tried spring break in the United States, I highly recommend it. It was a fever dream. We were living every moment for that moment.

Then, in the blink of an eye, just as we were gearing up to head back to campus, something happened that none of us could have predicted. A mysterious virus had triggered a global pandemic. Our phones blew up with emails: Campuses were shutting down. Schools were closing indefinitely. The COVID-19 virus hit the world hard and fast.

A CHOICE TO MAKE (by Alex)

We had two options: Either board the last flights back to France before international travel was suspended and finish school online—effectively ending our American journey—or stay put, trapped on an empty campus, attending classes online and waiting for the world to figure itself out so we could start playing soccer again.

Over the next couple of months, our international friends packed their bags and flew home. In fact, at Tom's school, by the time May rolled around, he was the only international student left on campus. But he wasn't ready to give up on soccer. Not yet. For Tom, this wasn't just a semester abroad—it was his shot at something bigger. He still believed in his dream of going pro, even with the injury. He had eligibility left, and he wasn't about to let a pandemic steal that from him. As for me? I was having way too much fun to go home and still had high hopes of one day playing professional soccer in the U.S.

So, we made our decision. Instead of going home, we were going to see more of this country. Travel had never been more affordable, and we were low risk, so I booked a ticket to meet Tom in Mississippi. Tom and I, a bubble of two, rented a car and threw a dart at a map. It landed in Diamondhead, Mississippi, a resort-style town close by, so that's where we went.

For our second destination, we decided to be more selective. We'd seen many TV shows and movies set in Charleston, South Carolina, and it came across as a beautiful city with an interesting culture. As luck would have it, the owner of an Airbnb on James Island made us an offer we couldn't refuse. He said he needed some painting done. If we could do the job for him, he would give us a free place to stay. How could we refuse?

We made Charleston our home for a little while, and we fell in love with it rapidly thanks to the good food, drinks, and beaches. It felt to us like a safe haven during those uncertain early days of the pandemic. That little house was also the place where we would start making videos together.

THE BEGINNING OF EVERYTHING (by Tom)

Like many of us during the pandemic, Alex and I spent a lot of time on social media. We noticed something: No one was talking about what it really felt like to be French in the U.S. The cultural quirks, the little moments of feeling like an alien, the way our Frenchness made us stand out—none of it was out there. Maybe people would be interested in hearing about that experience. Maybe they'd find it funny, or could even relate to what we went through. We weren't thinking in terms of starting a business or using it to earn a living, mind you. It was purely coming from a place where we thought some people might be entertained by our misadventures and point of view.

So, with a sense of fun and wonder, we created a social media account. A for Alex, T for Tom, and us being Frenchies = AT Frenchies.

Our first video was pure silliness: us on a Charleston beach, Alex playing an over-the-top American, all confidence and clichés, while I hammed it up as a bumbling Frenchman, tripping over cultural cues. We were bored, stuck in the middle of the pandemic, and honestly, just cracking ourselves up. There was no script, no strategy to go viral—just two guys leaning into our French roots with sarcasm and a wink.

Back then, Charleston was a bubble where COVID restrictions were loose, giving us the freedom to explore and create. So we kept it going, filming more videos as we wandered the colorful streets, poking fun at ourselves while discovering the city. Each clip was a snapshot of our lives: French guys navigating American quirks, from the local obsession with excessively sweetened iced tea to speed-walking the streets, with a dose of humor that felt like home. Our ideas were born from random moments—like joking about how Americans say "awesome" for everything while the French might just shrug, "C'est pas mal." We'd think, "Hey, that's funny," grab the phone, and hit record.

We were just two twentyish-year-olds, a bit restless, making each other laugh. But as we started sprinkling in more about French culture—phrases, habits—something clicked. People didn't just watch—they connected. Our videos, silly as they were, struck a chord. Maybe it was the authenticity, or the way we didn't care about looking polished or perfect. Or maybe everyone could relate to that feeling of being a fish out of water. Or just maybe this was the first inkling that our point of view was fresh enough and unique enough to offer something even more valuable to others.

Within two weeks, we had one hundred thousand followers. One hundred thousand! We were floored. It wasn't like we had a marketing degree or a viral playbook—we were just being ourselves, laughing at our own jokes, and sharing our French perspective.

If our first ten videos had flopped, we probably would've kept posting for the summer, just for kicks, then dropped it when school started. But the likes, comments, and messages poured in, with people saying, "This is so relatable!" or "Teach us more French!" People started asking for specific content—French phrases, cultural tips, even our takes on American fast food—and we rolled with it. We couldn't stop. People were hungry for what we were sharing. Why would we quit when it felt so right?

It hit me that we'd really done something special when, a few years later, we were contacted by the French embassy in the U.S., which had become aware of what we were doing. They invited us to the White House Correspondents' Dinner. We'd done other events by that point: partnerships with energy drinks, bottled water brands, popular language-learning apps, even the Cannes Film Festival. But this was a major political and celebrity gathering. And we were gathering there. Who the hell were we? What did that say about us? What were we learning about ourselves and about what we'd accomplished?

It was those thoughts that inspired us to put words on a page. Our journey from two lost French teenagers with broken dreams to accidental cultural ambassadors has taught us something profound: Sometimes the best path forward isn't the one you planned. It's the one that finds you when you're brave enough to approach life with a healthy curiosity about all things and stay open to possibility—everything the French way is about. We started out just trying to salvage our soccer careers and ended up building bridges between cultures, helping people find joy in learning French, and showing them a mentally healthier way to approach life.

This book isn't just about two French guys who stumbled into social media fame. It's about what got us there. It's about the power of resilience, the importance of staying true to yourself even when life throws you a curveball, and the unexpected ways that sharing your authentic story can impact others. From that makeshift soccer field in Canton to the White House Correspondents' Dinner, from whistled conversations with Coco to interviewing the French president (in English!), we've learned that every setback can lead to a comeback if you're willing to keep pushing forward.

Now, looking back, we see why it worked. It was never about chasing viral fame or copying trends. It was about being unapologetically us—two French guys, a little out of place, sharing our world with humor and heart. That's the French way: Live authentically, stay curious, bring smiles and warmth to people, and they will invite you in.

We're still those guys on the beach, goofing off, but now we're also storytellers, bridging cultures one sarcastic video at a time. And honestly? We're just getting started.

Part I

THE FRENCH MINDSET

COMMENT PENSER,
RESSENTIR ET BOUGER À LA FRANÇAISE

How to think, feel, and move through life the French way

Before you can live like the French, you have to *think* like the French. And no, that doesn't mean smoking on balconies, complaining about tourists, or arguing over which arrondissement has the best pastries (though, for the record, it's the sixth).

Thinking à la française is a state of mind. It's curiosity over chaos. Confidence without noise. Pleasure without guilt. It's knowing that doing less but doing it beautifully is an art form. We don't rush to the finish line. We stroll there, espresso in hand. We ask questions, challenge everything (including ourselves), and never confuse busyness with purpose. In France, the goal isn't to have it all. It's to *feel it all*—deeply, deliciously, deliberately.

The French mindset isn't about perfection; it's about presence. It's learning to stay open, protect your peace, take your time, and live in a way that actually feels like you. We don't perform life. We *live* it.

Before we dive into the parts of this book where we'll explain how to love, eat, and connect the French way, we start here at the foundation. The inner architecture. The mindset that makes everything else make sense.

Think of this as your mental reset. Your permission slip to stop rushing, stop hustling, and start savoring. Because once you master the way the French think, everything else, from the way you flirt to the way you order wine, just clicks into place.

Chapter 2.

CHOOSE CURIOSITY EVERY DAY

Avec Tom

"Why do Americans smile at strangers?" I texted Alex one afternoon while sitting in a Mississippi parking lot. I felt puzzled after someone waved at me as he passed, like we were old friends, despite our never having met before. In France, we reserve smiles for people who've earned them, or at the very least for people we actually know. I didn't want to shake the question off; I wanted to dig into it. Why the smiles, waves, and—even stranger—hugs for actual strangers? That tiny moment, that why, was curiosity in real time, the most French trait I didn't know I had.

If we could bottle up the French mindset into a single philosophy for success, it'd be this: Always stay curious. No matter how old you are, no matter where life takes you, there's always more to learn.

When I was in college in Mississippi, I had a lot of friends say stuff like, "I got an A, I've mastered it." But this never made sense to me, because in France our grading scale goes up to 20—and no one ever gets a perfect 20/20. Even in math, where you'd think a right answer is a right answer, the teachers will still find a way to dock you half a point for a wonky comma or a tiny glitch in your reasoning. Perfection? Doesn't exist.

It's the same outside of school. A lot of parents in the U.S. shower their kids with compliments—"You're the best, I'm so proud!"—which, don't get me wrong, is extremely nice. But French parents? Not really their style. That bubble burst early. If I scored five goals in a match, my dad wouldn't let a single missed pass slide. "Yeah, Tom, good game, but that corner kick? Sloppy." My mom? Same deal. "You scored, sure, but you weren't giving 100 percent."

This isn't mean. Just real and constructive. Parents aren't just a safety net in France—they are coaches, too. No coddling, no happy bubble. Always driving the details and pushing kids to fill in the blanks. There are always holes in your game, we're taught, even if they shrink over time. Honestly, I'm better for it. In the end, this is what pushed me to always look for ways to improve on the field, in school, and in life.

(If a French person ever tells you, "C'est pas mal?" *Not bad?* Take the win. That's about as high as praise gets. Telling someone who crushed it that it "wasn't bad"? That's French to the core.)

This chapter isn't about memorizing facts or collecting degrees—it's about embracing the French mindset of *rester curieux*, or staying curious like a child. This is the spark that drives all of us to pick up a new skill, explore a new culture, or ask "why" when everyone else has moved on.

Think of it this way: In France, curiosity isn't something you do. It's who you are. It's how you order drinks, how you debate politics, how you fall in love. The French ask questions not to get answers but to enjoy the space between them. We never "finish" learning. We just get more interesting while we do it. Every conversation, every mistake? Extra credit. We've distilled this mindset into nine rules to help you cultivate that same curiosity wherever you are.

RULE 1: LET CURIOSITY DRIVE YOUR AMBITION

The French have a quiet conviction: *La vie ne s'arrête jamais.* Life never stops. It stretches, evolves, shifts under your feet. And when you move with it (without trying to control it), you realize that learning isn't a luxury. It's survival. It's style.

That's why for us, success isn't about crossing a finish line. It's about motion, refinement, evolution, the subtle art of getting better without ever being done. There's always more to taste, to learn, to master. That's the ambition that keeps us alive.

But don't confuse it with pressure or perfectionism. *Oh mon Dieu, non.* (Oh my God, no.) We don't chase perfect. We flirt with it, knowing we'll never catch it. Because if perfection doesn't exist, then everything stays possible. That's freedom.

Our American friends like to say, "You people need therapy—learn to love yourselves!" And maybe they're right. But for us, this restless curiosity isn't self-loathing . . . it's self-respect. It's knowing there's always more to reach for, more to uncover.

We're never satisfied. Most French people aren't. We live in that delicious gap between who we are and who we could be. That tension—it's not stress; it's fuel.

Ambition, for us, isn't about admiration. That's more of an American pastime—the applause, the validation, the gold star. In France, ambition is quieter. It's personal. It's about growing for the sake of growth, becoming for the sake of becoming.

And if no one notices? Even better.

RULE 2: LEARN IN COMMUNITY

Curiosity doesn't just shape how we learn; it also shapes what we share. The more questions we asked our AT Frenchies community, the more we realized how many people around us were eager to understand French culture. Funny enough, that's when something unexpected happened.

One night, Alex and I had a few friends over when someone said, "You should start an online French school." My first thought was, "Are you serious? Who would want to learn from us?" But his enthusiasm was contagious.

"Trust me, it will work," he insisted.

After discussing it, we decided to give it a try. We'd noticed a growing desire from our community to learn French, but not in the traditional classroom. These were curious individuals, passionate about French culture but hesitant to be in a conventional classroom or sit through boring grammar drills. They wanted something real. And their curiosity? You could feel it. It was refreshing, and honestly, it reminded us of why we fell in love with all this in the first place.

So, we created the French Club, a space for our community to learn French through simple and easy-to-digest lessons. But what truly made the club unique wasn't the vocabulary or grammar we learned. It was the connection we built over time. Learning something new, especially as an adult, can feel overwhelming. You forget words, lose confidence, and suddenly find yourself back at the beginning. It's humbling. We wanted to change that. We stripped away the stress and made learning feel natural, even enjoyable. At the French Club, we keep things light, fun, and honest. No pressure to be perfect, no judgment if you say "le baguette" instead of "la baguette." Just a safe space where people feel seen, heard, and encouraged.

What surprised us most was the community that emerged. It wasn't just a group of people trying to pass a test. These were individuals who had a real, personal connection to French through family roots, a life-changing trip to France, or a deep love for the culture. For them, learning French was a way to reconnect with something meaningful.

That's when we realized: The French way is more than just language. It's a new perspective and worldview. The French language opens doors to a vast community stretching from Quebec to Senegal, from the Caribbean to Asia. It's a world many of us feel connected to, even without visiting these places. We're not just teaching; we're passing on that desire to keep growing, to keep exploring.

But perhaps most important, the French way is a mindset. A reminder that it's never too late to stay curious, and that learning doesn't have to stop once school ends. And the best part? Every time someone tells us, "I never thought I could learn a language, but now I actually enjoy it," we feel that same spark that got us into this in the first place. That's what French curiosity is all about—staying connected to the world, challenging yourself, and refusing to let time dull your sense of wonder.

RULE 3: SURPRISE YOURSELF

Back in grad school, my roommate Tiago had this quote he would repeat all the time: "Don't expect, be surprised." It stuck with me, and honestly, it might be the Frenchest thing I've ever heard (even though he was Portuguese, ha!).

We often think we can predict how things will go, but the reality is, we don't actually know anything for sure. And that's the beauty of life. Letting yourself be surprised by what happens if you try, by what happens if you follow your interest wherever it takes you—that's curiosity in action.

I learned this lesson the hard way when I attended my very first college class in the U.S. I walked in expecting to be able to keep up just fine. I had studied enough English to get in, right? Instead, I quickly realized that I didn't know nearly as much of the language as I thought. Words, expressions, even the way people communicated nonverbally were hard to grasp. I was completely lost.

At this time, Mattie, my girlfriend, became a huge part of this learning curve. I must have asked her a billion times to do my homework for me because it would have been an easy A. She is super smart, she speaks English perfectly, and my classes were too easy for her. Meanwhile, I could barely put three sentences together. But she *always* refused. Instead, she pushed me to do it myself, promising to read my work afterward and explain the mistakes. In the moment, it felt like a punishment and a waste of time, but now I can honestly say it's the reason I learned English so quickly, and the reason I started to love using and learning this language so much.

Fast-forward a few years, and I was writing thirty-page papers every month for my master's degree. On my own. No shortcuts. No cheating. Just the result of asking questions, staying curious, and letting myself be surprised by how much I could learn when I actually tried. If Mattie had just handed me the answers, I never would have taken pride in my work, and I would have missed out on proving to myself what I was capable of.

So now I believe this more than ever: Anyone can do anything if they put their mind to it. Like Tiago would say, "Don't expect, be surprised"—especially by how far your curiosity can take you.

L'histoire d'Alex (Alex's Story)

Feed Your Joy

In college, my professor once told me, "You study too much." It was the first and only time I ever heard that in my life. He meant it as a compliment, but I took it as a warning: Curiosity should feed joy, not ego. Since then I've studied everything with one rule: If it doesn't make me smile, it's not worth the test.

RULE 4: LET CURIOSITY LEAD, NOT EGO

The French don't learn to impress—they learn because the world is too fascinating to ignore. When we started the French Club, we weren't experts; we were just curious about sharing our culture. That curiosity led to late nights researching, experimenting with video formats, and learning from our community's feedback. My dad used to say, "Curiosity never retires," and we see this play out in everyone from our neighbor, who at sixty-eight is teaching herself Japanese, to our friend's little brother, who quizzes everyone about constellations.

Check your ego at the door: Pick something you know nothing about—a language, a craft, a history—and dive in. You don't need to be good; you just need to be open. The joy is in the discovery, not the spotlight.

L'histoire d'Alex

Verify, Verify, Verify

I'm a stats nerd. It's just one of my many quirks, but my friends always tease me about it. They're like, "Alex, you're always digging deeper into something." If someone drops a fact at dinner or in a text, I'm not just nodding along—I'm

pulling out my phone, ready to research. "You say that's true? Cool, I'm checking." It's not that I don't trust people. Even when my girlfriend, whom I trust with my heart, says, "Did you hear about that political drama today?" I'll listen, intrigued, but still dive into the details myself. I need to know the facts are *solide*, especially in this wild world where fake news spreads like crazy.

You see, there's so much noise out there—people getting their "news" from overheard train chats, their eccentric aunt, or some random social media post. I'm a talker, obviously. I love to chat, debate, share stories—so I want to make sure what I'm saying holds up. If I'm repeating something, you can trust it's been vetted.

This curiosity, this need to verify, it's not a flaw—it's a superpower. Like the French mindset, it's about staying hungry to learn, to grow, to never just swallow what's fed to you. In today's world, with misinformation swirling like a storm, checking your sources is how you stay sharp and keep the conversation authentic.

Take the U.S., for example. Here, the First Amendment—freedom of speech and press—is sacred and beautiful, yet it can be messy. You hear one story on one channel, a completely different one on another. In France, we're lucky to have strict laws keeping news outlets in check, pushing for balance, slicing through bias like a knife through brie.

Of course, I'm still learning, always. Curiosity isn't a checkbox; it's a lifestyle. So, *mes amis*, take a cue from this Frenchman: Next time someone drops a "fact," don't just nod—dig. Check the stats, read the source, and ask why. This isn't to prove anyone wrong necessarily but to keep your

mind as vibrant as a Parisian café, buzzing with ideas and truth. That's how you stay curious, stay relevant, and some might say . . . wise.

RULE 5: EMBRACE THE BEGINNER'S MINDSET

Starting over is humbling, but the French see it as strength. That's the French way: No age, no stage is too late to begin. We feel it now as we're visiting new countries and learning about different cultures—fumbling with etiquette, laughing at our attempts with the language, but loving the process of exploration.

We also saw it over and over in our French Club. Seventy-four-year-old Kate was one of our students who started her journey feeling unsure. One day, during class, she broke down in tears, asking herself if it was too late to learn. We took the time to reassure her, to show her how far she'd already come, the words she could now pronounce, the confidence she was beginning to build. And the next day, she came back with a spark in her eye, ready to keep going.

"I'm not giving up, I'm just getting started," she told us with a smile.

That moment stayed with me. Kate wasn't just trying to learn French; she was challenging herself. She reminded me that it's never too late to learn and grow, that growth in and of itself is the reward.

So next time you're scared to start something new, channel your inner Kate. Pick something you're interested in. Take a class, watch a tutorial, make a mess, and don't worry when you mess up. Being a beginner isn't failure. It's courage.

RULE 6: SEE MISTAKES AS TEACHERS, NOT SETBACKS

In France, mistakes aren't the end—they're the beginning of something new. Our teachers never let us fear a wrong answer; they'd say, "*Bon*, now what can we learn from this?" Next time you mess up, don't hide; rather, ask, "What's this showing me?" Mistakes are just curiosity in disguise, pointing you toward growth.

RULE 7: CONNECT YOUR LEARNING TO SOMETHING BIGGER

In France, learning is a shared journey, not a race. When we launched our online French school, it wasn't about outdoing other programs—it was about connecting with people who loved French culture. Anyone who has ever taught anything knows there is no better way to learn than to teach—that's, of course, if you're a good teacher. By building the learning process out to include others, you expand not only your reach but also your own opportunity for growth. Our students, from Quebec to California, brought stories of family roots or dream trips to Paris, turning lessons into conversations. I remember a student, Miguel, who learned French to read his grandmother's old letters. His joy wasn't in the grade he got but in the connection he forged to his family.

Try this: Whatever you're learning, do it alongside others. Join a book club, take a cooking class, or study with a friend. Share your questions and mistakes—it's how you grow deeper, together.

Think about it: Here we are, writing a book about our own culture; meanwhile, we are learning more about our own culture in the process! We encourage you to do the same. Is there a piece of your own cultural heritage you have both embraced and explored? That likely means, no matter how much you know, there's more to learn. And since you already have a passion for it, seek out new avenues for learning about your own heritage. It brings with it a kind of self-awareness that's hard to duplicate otherwise.

L'histoire d'Alex

Learning Is Best While Traveling

For some, travel is all about sprawling on a beach, cocktail in hand, melting into the sun like ice cream on a hot day. And there's nothing wrong with that—sipping a piña colada in the Bahamas is a beautiful thing. But for me, for us French, travel is a chance to dive into the soul of a place, to learn, grow, and come back with stories that make your friends lean in at the dinner table. It's about approaching the world with wide eyes, ready to uncover something new about a culture, a region—or even yourself.

I went to Morocco recently, expecting to soak up the souks, the spices, the colors of Marrakech. But I ended up learning more about my own French culture than I ever expected. I visited the Yves Saint Laurent Museum. It was incredible, and can you believe I had no idea that Saint Laurent worked under Christian Dior early in his career? Me, a Parisian, who grew up thinking I knew about the fashion world from growing up around it. But no, it took a trip to Morocco to school me. The museum didn't just show me Saint Laurent's genius; it showed how Moroccan architecture, textiles, and colors inspired his work, which then rippled back into French fashion. I came home understanding Paris a little better, seeing how our culture weaves into the world's tapestry.

That's the magic of travel—it's a mirror and a window. You learn about the place you're in, but you also discover pieces of your own story. Morocco taught me about Berber patterns, yes, but also about how global French fashion really is. It was humbling, and it made me grateful. I realized how lucky I was to come from a culture that's both a creator and a collector of the world's beauty.

Next time you plan a trip, think French. Sure, book a day or two to lounge by the sea, but then go deeper. Wander a local market, visit a museum, hike a trail that tests you. Talk to someone who lives there, ask about their life. Let yourself feel a little out of place—it's where the best lessons hide. Like my Morocco adventure, you'll come back richer, not just in memories but in who you are. That's travel, à la française: a journey to learn, to love, and to live a little bigger.

RULE 8: MAKE LEARNING A DAILY RITUAL

The French weave learning into our days like it's second nature. We'll dive into a history book before bed not for a test but because we love it. We will constantly pick up new skills—video editing, cultural research—not because we're forced but because when curiosity takes the lead, you follow.

Try making learning a part of your day. You don't have to take big steps either: Listen to a new podcast on your commute about a subject you know nothing about, attempt a new recipe, or learn five words in a new language. Make curiosity a habit, like brushing your teeth. Small, daily doses add up to a life of growth.

Here are a few other ideas:

- **Read One Article a Day About Something New.** Kickstart your day with a quick read on a topic outside your usual orbit—maybe urban gardening, AI ethics, or ancient mythology. Apps or newsletters make it easy to find bite-sized pieces in as little as five to ten minutes. When time is tight, this keeps your mind expansive without overwhelming your schedule. Bonus: It gives you fresh conversation fodder for happy hour.

- **Learn Five Words a Week in a New Language.** Inspired by the French Club's approach to making language learning fun, pick a language that intrigues you—Spanish, Mandarin, or hello . . . French—and make a goal to learn five words a week. Use a translation app to keep it super easy and just jot them down during a quick mind break.

- **Ask "Why."** Channel the French knack for questioning by asking "Why?" in regard to something you take for granted—why your team uses that software, why your partner loves that band, or why your city's traffic is so wild. You'll learn something unexpected, guaranteed. Even just asking it once can challenge your assumptions and deepen your understanding—or perhaps spur you to make a change.

- **Join a Group Class (Virtual or In-Person).** Join an astrology club, cooking class, or online photography group—something that meets regularly, either once a week or once a month, to fit your packed schedule. For those in blasé routines, this is a chance to connect while picking up a skill. It's less about mastering the activity and more about the stories and ideas you swap.

- **Try a New Tangible Skill.** Cooking a new dish or tackling a small DIY project—like making sourdough or painting a portrait of your cat—mirrors the French love for hands-on learning. When life feels serious, this brings playful experimentation. Pick something every two weeks to keep it doable. You'll mess up (burnt bread, anyone?), but as we've been saying, mistakes teach. Plus, you might impress your friends with a new skill.
- **Listen to Podcasts.** Podcasts are like the French café debates we love—rich with ideas and stories. Choose one episode a day or week on a topic you're curious about, from history to psychology to pop culture. We love podcasts during commutes or gym sessions. It's a low-effort way to absorb knowledge.

RULE 9: SHARE WHAT YOU LEARN TO DEEPEN IT

The French love sharing knowledge—it's why our gatherings turn into debates about art, history, or politics. When we started the French Club, teaching French deepened our own understanding of the language and culture. Sharing cements what you've learned and spreads the spark.

So share what you're learning. Teach a friend the new

craft you've picked up, write a blog post, or have everyone read an article and discuss it over dinner. This isn't about showing off but about making the knowledge your own and passing on this culture of curiosity. Don't be afraid to bring up something controversial either. If you do it from a place of learning with an eye toward good humor, nothing is off the table.

If you're trepidatious or unsure of just how to make this work, try to keep these tips on navigating French conversation in mind:

- **Debate = Connection, Not Conflict.** The French thrive on intellectual sparring. Disagreeing openly isn't rude; it's a sign you're engaged. Don't confuse passion with hostility.
- **Honesty Over Politeness.** Americans tend to soften opinions ("That's interesting, but . . ."). The French value blunt clarity. A sharp critique is often more respected than a sugar-coated half-truth.
- **Wit Is a Form of Respect.** Wordplay, irony, and clever comebacks are prized. A quick, witty remark signals you're present, mentally agile, and open to the humorous side of even tough, complex issues.
- **Don't Be Afraid of "Serious" Topics.** Politics, philosophy, literature, and world affairs are totally fair game, even over a casual coffee. Shying away can come off as disinterest.
- **Depth Beats Breadth.** In conversation, it's better to explore one idea thoroughly than skim many topics.

Lingering on a single subject shows appreciation for nuance.

- **Intellectual Curiosity Is Attractive.** Ask questions not just to be polite but because you're genuinely curious. Showing knowledge—or eagerness to learn—is a compliment.
- **Passion Is Not Taboo.** Raise your voice, gesture, argue energetically—these are all acceptable. Passion equals sincerity.
- **Humor Is Dry and Dark.** Don't expect big smiles or constant laughter. French humor often leans satirical, ironic, or self-deprecating. It's a "knowing smile" culture, not a "loud belly laugh" one.
- **Privacy Coexists with Openness.** They may dive into politics with you, but never ask how much money you make. Certain personal details (salary, work achievements, health) are private; intellectual life is public.
- **Don't Fear Silence.** Pauses are natural, even comfortable. The French don't feel the need to "fill the space" as many Americans do. Take the time to process and think before speaking.

Curiosity is not a phase. It's a way of living. The French way reminds us that learning is never about proving yourself or checking a box—it's about keeping your mind awake, your spirit flexible, and your heart open. Whether it's debating politics over coffee, fumbling through a new recipe, or learning a new language at seventy years old, the point isn't perfection. It's presence. It's having the courage to ask, to try, to laugh at your mistakes, and to keep going anyway.

To stay curious like a child is to accept that life is unfinished by design. The French embrace that imperfection not as failure but as freedom—freedom to grow, to question, to be ambitious, to connect more deeply with others and with ourselves. When we shift from chasing admiration to chasing knowledge, we discover that the real reward of curiosity is not mastery but discovery. It's the spark that keeps conversations alive, cultures vibrant, and our own lives endlessly expanding.

So take the win when someone tells you, "Pas mal." (Not bad . . . but in a good way.) It means you're on the path. The French don't chase answers; we collect better questions. That's how life stays interesting.

Chapter 3.

PROTECT YOUR PRIVATE LIFE

Avec Tom

There was a knock at the door. Not a loud one. The hesitant kind that makes you wish you'd pretended not to hear it. In France, surprise visits are rare, borderline scandalous. My parents would have whispered, "*Who dares?*" and tiptoed away from the door like we were hiding from the authorities.

Then came America, land of the casual drop-in. In college, I lived with roommates who thought doors were more of a suggestion than a boundary. People just appeared, friends of friends, sometimes total strangers, raiding the fridge, collapsing on the couch, staying the night like it was no big deal. I didn't mind it. I was just . . . taken aback. The freedom was disarming, almost endearing. In France, a surprise visitor feels like an intrusion. In the States, it feels like an invitation—to connection, to community, to letting life in without warning.

It struck me that this openness wasn't careless—it was cultural. The French protect privacy like art, Americans treat connection like oxygen.

That's when it hit me: Privacy, for the French, isn't secrecy. It's elegance. Protecting your private life doesn't mean hiding. It means curating who and what you let in emotionally, physically, digitally.

When I was growing up in France, I never thought much about our way of life. Alex and I lived like everyone else around us—no comparison, no analysis; it just was what it was. The exception, of course, was the U.S. Its influence was everywhere: the movies, the music, the idea that life was bigger, louder, somehow shinier. We admired it from afar but assumed, naively, that most of the world is more or less like us.

Spoiler alert: It isn't.

That illusion cracked the moment I noticed how differently people treated privacy abroad. In France, it's woven into daily life, an unspoken code we all obey without question. We're private with our emotions, our spaces, even our ambitions. Back home, intimacy is something you *earn*. It's not handed out like free Wi-Fi.

Your private life—meaning your home, your heart, your thoughts—is all sacred. To share everything is to cheapen it. To share selectively is to make it meaningful. Who you let in, whether into your home or your head, says everything about who you are.

We take that seriously—*maybe too seriously*, according to our American friends—but there's wisdom in the caution. What's yours is you.

The older I get, the more I realize privacy isn't about isolation. It's about intention. It's knowing when to open the door and when to let the knock fade into silence. Every culture has its rhythm of closeness, and the French one just happens to move a little slower, a little quieter. But once you're in, you're in for life. There's a kind of grace to that. A quiet confidence that doesn't need to perform connection to prove it exists. And maybe that's the lesson worth exporting.

So how do the French pull it off without becoming complete hermits? Simple. We follow a few quiet rules.

RULE 1: BOUNDARIES ARE A LUXURY

Step into a French home and you'll feel it instantly. *Bienvenue*—but tread lightly. There's an unspoken rhythm to what's shared, what's off-limits, and how to move through someone's private world without overstepping. You don't help yourself in the fridge—in fact, you don't even go into the kitchen. You certainly don't walk around someone's home by yourself. It's not about snobbery or secrecy. It's about intention. Because the way you treat your space and the way you move through someone else's reveals more about your character than any conversation could.

In France, no one just drops by. Spontaneity might look adorable on a show like *Friends*, but in real life, it's chaos. A French home is a sanctuary, not a social drive-through. Visits are planned, thoughtful, and deliberate—an event, not an interruption. And when someone does come over, they don't arrive empty-handed. They bring a candle, fresh flowers, a special treat. Small gestures mean everything.

For us, hospitality begins long before the door opens. We'll plan to make sure we have your favorite snacks or drinks on hand. We'll tidy up and put things we don't intend to share away in a drawer. We protect our peace and design our home (and our boundaries) with intention.

Try it: Don't wait for exhaustion to define your limits. Set them early, and kindly. If hosting a dinner party, tell your guests the starting and ending times in advance. Put away anything you don't want touched or seen. If someone stops by unexpectedly and you're too tired or busy to receive them, don't be afraid to let the doorbell ring, or keep the interaction brief and contained to the entryway. Just because someone wants to come in doesn't mean you have to let them.

True elegance isn't about pleasing everyone—it's about being at ease with yourself in your home. And your home is sacred.

RULE 2: LEAVE A LITTLE MYSTERY

Americans love a grand tour: "Here's the kitchen! Here's where the cat throws up!" In France, *non.* You're shown the spaces that matter: the entry, the dining room, maybe the kitchen if you've made the inner circle. Bedrooms and offices? Strictly private unless offered.

Privacy to us isn't secrecy. It's sensual. It's what keeps connection alive. Mystery isn't withholding; it's *inviting.* Not everything in life needs to be on display. Let people wonder a little. Keep a few doors closed when you have visitors over—literally and figuratively.

You don't need to be an open book to be understood. Sometimes, the most intriguing stories are the ones left partly unread.

RULE 3: OBSERVE BEFORE YOU ENTER

Respect, for us, lives in the details—how you cross a threshold, what you notice when you do. If your host is barefoot, you take your shoes off. If they're in dress shoes, you probably keep yours on. You read the room.

Boundaries often whisper before they speak. The art of awareness is noticing without assuming, adapting without overcompensating. Those small acts—waiting, observing, adjusting—build harmony faster than any polite "merci" ever could.

RULE 4: BE WARM, NOT INVASIVE

French hospitality is inviting but never unrestrained. We love a lively conversation but not a confessional. Oversharing too soon, or asking too much too fast, feels like emotional trespassing. We prefer conversations that linger, not unravel. Talk about ideas, travel, art, music—anything that stirs the mind. The French don't fear depth; we just like to arrive there slowly. Curiosity is magnetic. Interrogation is exhausting.

RULE 5: OPEN THE DOOR— BUT ON YOUR TERMS

Privacy isn't a prison. We're not suggesting you become hermits guarding your homes like royal archives. We've known people like that—trust us, it's overrated. Growing up, we could count on one hand how many friends ever crossed our doorstep. Our parents believed that keeping our space sacred was safety.

Then we moved to the U.S.—and fell head over heels for American openness: the invitations, the shared meals, the easy warmth of letting people in. It felt vulnerable and beautiful. We learned to blend both worlds: to host warmly but selectively, to share generously but never out of obligation.

That's the real art of boundaries—knowing when to say yes, when to say no, and when to say *not yet.*

You owe no one access to your space or your story. But you also owe yourself the joy of connection. Choose both—intentionally.

Treat homes like sanctuaries. Treat people like art. And treat your privacy like perfume—worn close to the skin, never poured out for everyone to smell.

The beauty of boundaries is that once you master them in your space, they start shaping everything else—your pace, your patience, your presence. A calm home creates a calm mind. And when life feels intentional, you stop chasing time and start savoring it.

Which brings us to the next lesson: how to make time feel like a luxury instead of a race.

Chapter 4.

REDEFINE THE HUSTLE

Avec Alex

It happened over lunch—a long one, naturally. I was back in Paris after a year in the States, sitting at a tiny café in Saint-Germain, the kind with tables so small you have to angle your glass of wine to make room for the bread basket. The air smelled like butter, espresso, and a little bit of nostalgia.

My friend lingered over her dessert, calm as a cat in the sun. I, on the other hand, was quietly spiraling. The check hadn't come. The waiter had vanished. Ten minutes passed. Then twenty. I didn't have anywhere to be, but that didn't seem to matter. There was this low hum in my chest, that familiar American urgency feeling like an invisible clock was whispering, *Move along, move along.* What was taking so long?

My friend looked at me, amused. "Relax," she said. "He'll bring it when he brings it."

And that's when it hit me: *I'd gone full American*. Somewhere between New York and Los Angeles, I'd forgotten the ability to wait without fidgeting. I'd mistaken stillness for inefficiency. I'd lost my chill.

In France, waiting isn't a waste. It's part of the experience. The meal isn't finished until the conversation is. The check doesn't arrive until . . . well, until it does. Time isn't managed. It's respected. It isn't something you dominate. It's something you dance with. We don't try to bend it, beat it, or color-code it. We move *with* it, like a partner who knows when to lead and when to let go.

Slowing down isn't about doing less. It's about doing things *well*. It's giving your moments the same care you'd give a meal, a friendship, or a good sentence. When you slow down, life doesn't stop. It deepens.

We're not superheroes of serenity. We've just stopped treating time like an enemy to conquer. The French don't hack their calendars or chase balance. We let it find us. A few quiet habits keep our days feeling rich instead of rushed, and they start with knowing when to stop.

RULE 1: DON'T CONFUSE MOTION WITH PROGRESS

Let's talk about the addiction nobody wants to quit: *hustle*. We've seen it—the glorified exhaustion, the bragging about eighty-hour weeks, inbox heroics, caffeine as personality. It's an entire aesthetic of burnout.

We see this and think, *pitié* (pity). In France, we don't worship exhaustion; we nap through it. We take our five weeks of paid vacation (not a measly two) and actually use them. We log off at 6 p.m., protected by laws that guarantee the right to disconnect. No midnight emails, no performative grind. Work stays at work and life takes center stage.

Rest isn't a reward for working hard. It's a requirement for working *well*. Claim your weekends. Protect your evenings. Take a nap like it's your civic duty. You're not being indulgent; you're being strategic. When you rest, you recharge. You return sharper, calmer, more creative. You come back with something hustle alone can't give you: clarity.

Try this: Once this week, stop midday and do nothing for ten minutes. Not scrolling, not multitasking. Just *being*. Notice how uncomfortable it feels—that's your nervous system detoxing from urgency.

RULE 2: TREAT TIME LIKE WINE, NOT WATER

Americans treat time like water. They gulp it down, measure it by the ounce, and brag about their daily intake. It's a resource to manage, ration, and optimize. The French? We treat time like wine—something to sip, swirl, and savor. You don't chug Bordeaux from a plastic bottle; you let it breathe, you taste it. You make a ritual of it.

Some people love efficiency. There's pride in optimization, shaving minutes, stacking tasks, turning life into a spreadsheet. But time isn't money. It's more fragile than that. You can always make more money. You'll never make more time.

In France, we treat time like a sensory experience. We sit in it. We stretch it. We know the best things in life take their sweet time. You can taste it in our long lunches, where conversation lingers after the plates are cleared. You can feel it in the two-hour dinners, where no one's in a rush to order dessert. And you can see it in the way we walk—not rushing, not dawdling, just *present.*

If you treat every moment like an investment, you'll miss the interest: joy. Slow time is the secret ingredient to meaning.

Next time you're with someone, resist the urge to check your phone. Or better yet, don't bring it. Okay, we might not be ready for that one. Let's go slow—just keep it in your bag or put it face down on the table. But you get what we're saying: Let the moment expand by being present in it. Pretend time doesn't belong to anyone—especially not your notifications.

RULE 3: SAYING NO IS AN ART

A big part of savoring time is knowing when you don't have it, or when something—an ask, an event, a project—or someone is not worth it. That's when it's time to say no.

The French *non* is never cold. It's clear. It's the velvet rope around your peace. Americans treat no like rejection. We treat it like refinement. Every *non* creates space and time for something that actually belongs.

Early on, we said yes to everything—every brand, every collaboration, every half-fit opportunity that "might lead somewhere." Fact: It mostly led to burnout. Now when we say yes, it's because it aligns with our beliefs or passions, and it's something we can authentically get behind. And as a result, it becomes much more meaningful to not only us but our followers, too.

Saying *non* doesn't limit your life. It defines it. Every time you refuse what's wrong for you, you make time for what's right for you.

RULE 4: MASTER THE ART OF DOING NOTHING

Don't have any free time because you're too busy? That's your choice. Make some.

In France, we practice *flânerie*—the art of wandering without purpose, just curiosity. It's the opposite of grinding. We stroll the long way home. We sit on a bench and watch the world move. We people-watch like it's a film.

A lot of people we know tend to treat leisure as a luxury. The French see it as maintenance, like brushing your teeth or drinking water. You don't skip it. Doing nothing isn't laziness; it's compost for creativity. When you step away from the noise, your mind stretches and your spirit exhales.

Try this: Take the long route home, whether walking or driving. Listen to your favorite artist. Enjoy a podcast. Or just enjoy the ride itself. Don't track it, don't post it, don't justify it. Wander until something (or nothing) catches your attention. That's the point.

RULE 5: PLEASURE BEFORE PRODUCTIVITY

Pleasure isn't a side dish to Parisians; it's the meal. We don't earn it; we expect it. People often think joy comes *after* the hard work. The French think it's what makes the work worth doing in the first place.

Start small. Light a candle, even if you're dining alone. Bake cookies, even if they're just for you. Drink the good stuff on a regular Tuesday. Take the long shower, play the loud music, walk without a destination. Pleasure doesn't require perfection—only permission. So once a day, ask yourself, *What would make this moment more enjoyable?* Then do it. Simple as that.

And here's the twist: When you prioritize pleasure, you actually get *more* done. Because you're not dragging yourself through the day like a martyr. You're fueled by something far more sustainable: joy.

RULE 6: VALUE THE PROCESS, NOT THE PAYOFF

"I had a super-productive morning." "I squeezed in another call." Simmer down! Treat your productivity like air: You breathe it, not measure it. The French care more about *how* something's done than *how fast*. In work, that means obsession with detail—not for perfection but for integrity. It's what turns a task into a craft.

We learned this the hard way while filming videos for the French Club. When we rushed, the content was fine—but flat. When we slowed down, laughed between takes, and let the rhythm roll naturally, it suddenly felt alive again.

RULE 7: FIND YOUR RHYTHM

Everyone talks about "finding balance" like it's this holy state of calm, a perfectly even life where nothing tips too far in any direction. But that's not balance. That's boredom. Real balance isn't about standing still. It's about staying in rhythm.

Life has a beat. Some days it's bass-heavy chaos, other days it's a soft acoustic loop. The trick isn't to keep the same tempo, it's to *feel* when to shift. The French get this instinctively. We don't treat our pace like something to perfect. We let it roll. We lean in when life speeds up, and when it slows, we don't fight it. We glide.

Still, that mindset doesn't come naturally when you're building something from scratch, like a business or side gig. There's this seductive voice that says, *Keep going. Don't stop. You can rest later.* We've heard it, we've believed it, and we've crashed because of it.

At one point, we thought the goal was endurance. That the harder we pushed, the faster we'd get "there." Spoiler: There is no *there*. There's only you, the work, and how much you can give before you start running on fumes.

It took a wake-up call—a very French one, actually—to

remind us that stopping isn't weakness, and that finding the right rhythm is the key to great work.

I'll let Tom tell you how we learned this the hard way.

L'histoire de Tom

Sprint vs. Recovery

When Alex and I were pouring our hearts into launching the French Club, our online French language learning platform, the weeks leading up to the big day were a whirlwind. Everything needed to be created from scratch. We were designing every feature, planning every lesson, filming videos, posting stories, replying to messages, and tweaking every detail to make sure it felt right. It was exciting, but also intense. Our entire days revolved around it.

About a month before the launch, we were in overdrive, chasing perfection—or at least as close as we could get to it. I was staying with my parents, and my routine was relentless: wake up, work, eat, work, eat, work, sleep, repeat. No breaks, no pauses, just the grind.

One evening, my dad pulled me aside, his voice calm but serious.

"Tom, you need to rest," he said, leaning against the kitchen counter. "You can't just work nonstop. You and Alex, you're burning yourselves out. You need a day off—a real one. Pick a Saturday or Sunday and do nothing. No emails, no social media, no French Club. Just rest." He raised an eyebrow, the way he does when he's about to make a point. "Why do you think people have weekends? Even in a nine-to-five, Monday to Friday is work, and Saturday, Sunday are for living. You need that space to breathe."

I pushed back right away. "I'm not in a nine-to-five, Papa. I'm building something with Alex. If I stop, it all stops—there's no one else to pick up the slack. Alex and I kind of *have* to keep going." I meant it. I was young, brimming with energy, and honestly, I felt like I could power through it.

"I'd rather push and grind now," I told him, "so later, I won't have to hustle as hard as everyone else. I can handle it." But he didn't buy it.

"That's how you burn out," he said. "You're not a machine."

My mom didn't say much at first, but later that night, she sat next to me on the sofa and said quietly, "I know you're focused. I see how much this matters to you. I'm not asking you to stop now, but when this big push is over, take a real break. It will help you do better and go even further afterward." It wasn't a lecture. She just understood the rhythm I was in and found a way to help me realize that recovery wasn't optional. It was fuel to make our work better.

That moment with my parents got me thinking deeply about work-life balance and how it's not one-size-fits-all. In France, we're taught to value life outside work—long lunches, evenings with friends, time to just *be*. But when you're building something like the French Club, the lines blur. There's no clocking out at 5 p.m., no tidy weekends. At the time, we were in launch mode—there was no such thing as balance. It wasn't just Alex and me either. Our whole team, while small, was in overdrive, working around the clock to make this thing happen. To this day, running the French Club means there's rarely a day we can fully check out. Some days are lighter—maybe just a few emails or brainstorming over coffee—but when we're in an intense season, like that prelaunch sprint, it's all hands on deck, every single day.

But it's not always like that. Some weeks now are much quieter. Like this one, for example—I've been writing for this book, brainstorming content, going to the gym, actually cooking meals instead of just grabbing whatever was easiest, even taking naps. It's still work, but it feels manageable. I've got time to breathe, to live. I'm not stuck in that "eat-work-eat" loop.

Our rhythm isn't linear. It changes with the seasons of our work. There are sprints, and then there's recovery. My dad's French instincts caught us midsprint, when everything looked chaotic, and immediately sent up red flags for him. He did not see the calm that followed.

Still, my parents' words stuck: Rest isn't a luxury, it's a necessity. For some, balance means working five days and taking two off, like a classic nine-to-five. For others, it's three weeks of intense focus followed by a week to recharge. For Alex and me, it's about riding the waves—diving in when the work demands it, then pulling back to rest when the storm passes.

The key is finding what works for *you* and honoring it. Balance isn't about splitting your time perfectly but about making space for both the hustle and the quiet so you can keep going without burning out. That launch taught me we could push hard, but it also showed me that rest afterward is what keeps the fire alive.

RULE 8: DON'T WASTE YOUR TIME NOT BEING *YOU*

Your time is too precious to spend it being anything other than yourself. This is one of the most important lessons we've learned, and it came along as things often do—with an email.

We were maybe a year into creating the French Club, still juggling side gigs, eating pasta four nights a week, and praying our Wi-Fi didn't crash mid-livestream when a major brand slid into our inbox. Let's just say it rhymed with "Schmenergy Schmink." They wanted us to promote their "hydration elixir," a glossy bottle of electrolytes, antioxidants, and marketing poetry. The pitch promised to "embody balance and vitality."

Translation: *We'll pay you a ton of money to pretend you drink this every morning.*

Tom and I looked at each other, trying not to grin. This was a huge paycheck. For one post. We'd never been offered that many digits before. For anything.

"Easy," Tom said. "We could shoot it tomorrow."

I raised an eyebrow. "Do you even drink that stuff?"

"No," he admitted. "But I could start."

We filmed a test video anyway. The lighting was perfect, the script polished, the smiles just a little too bright. Watching it back, something felt off. It wasn't us. The tone, the words, the energy . . . it reeked of pretending.

We both sat in silence. Then I sighed. "We can't post this, right?"

"No," Tom said. "We can't."

So we didn't. We turned down the money, deleted the footage, and ate our pasta like broke philosophers.

That night, Tom raised his glass of tap water and toasted, "To authenticity."

We laughed it off, but I felt something click. The relief of saying *non* was instant—like taking off shoes that never fit. That's when I realized: The true luxury isn't success; it's alignment. It's choosing to spend your time doing what aligns with your values, with who you really are.

That moment taught us something we'd somehow forgotten: Success means nothing if it costs you yourself. In France, that's not just philosophy; it's self-preservation. Authenticity is the ultimate status symbol. Everything else—clothes, cars, looks—fades.

That's why the French take forever to commit—to jobs, homes, even haircuts. We're not indecisive; we're deliberate. We don't chase what glitters. We wait for what fits. Because when the applause fades, you'll be left alone with your choices, and authenticity echoes loudest in silence.

A French clockmaker once said, "A watch is only as honest as its smallest gear." That line stayed with me. You can polish the face, wind it daily, make it sparkle—but if one tiny piece inside is out of sync, it will always tell the wrong time.

People are no different. Authenticity is your internal

mechanism, the quiet alignment between who you are, what you do, and what you stand for. You can fake success for a while. But misalignment ticks louder with time.

So recalibrate. Listen for the click. Tighten what's loose. Oil what's stuck. Because when everything inside you moves in harmony, you stop racing the clock—and start keeping time with yourself.

Our philosophy on savoring life and taking our time seeps into everything we do. It's the French mindset: Live deeply, notice the little things, and stop treating peace like a prize you earn. After seven years in the U.S., we've absorbed some American drive, too. We love to build, to push, to dream big. But we've learned that ambition without grace is just noise, and that success is measured not by how busy we are but by how honest our lives feel. When what you do finally matches who you are, you stop chasing meaning—and start living it.

So here's your permission slip: Walk slower, linger longer, order dessert, take the nap, miss the email. Say no to the things that don't align with who you really are. Make time for being authentically *you*. The world won't slow down for you, but you can choose to move differently inside it.

Time isn't running out. It's unfolding. And the art of living well is knowing when to stop rushing—and start enjoying your precious life.

Part II

LIVING À LA FRANÇAISE

ENTRE LA TÊTE ET LE CŒUR

Between the head and the heart

By now you've hopefully got the mindset down. You've learned to stay curious, guard your peace, set your pace, and live like you mean it.

Bravo. You're officially fluent in chill.

Now comes the real art: *living it out in your day-to-day.* Because being French isn't just a way of thinking. It's a way of being. It's not about logic. It's about rhythm, intuition, texture, and the choices you make along the way.

It's how we approach a first date: simple, low-key, no theatrics. Just two people, good conversation, and the possibility of something real.

It's how we linger long after the dessert, savoring the moment instead of rushing toward an exit.

It's how we reach for timeless pieces over trends, letting quiet elegance do the heavy lifting while we pretend it took no effort at all.

We say *entre la tête et le cœur* (between the head and the heart) because the magic lives right there, in the tension between sense and sensitivity. Logic keeps you steady; emotion gives you flavor. Without one, you're either chaos or cardboard.

So let them flirt. Live in the in-between.

Let reason hold hands with romance.

Let ambition dance with joy.

Let boundaries make room for belonging.

The next chapters are about that dance. How to love, eat, argue, flirt, and connect à la française. This is where philosophy becomes pleasure.

So pour yourself something—tea, espresso, or something stronger; we won't judge. Take a long breath. Loosen your jaw. Let your shoulders drop. Because from here on out, it's not about how to *feel* like a French person—it's about how to *live* like one.

Chapter 5.

LOVE BOLDLY

Avec Alex

Back home in France, people fall into love as if they're sinking into a long, detailed novel—slowly, easily, no neon signs shouting, "This is it!" Like a great mystery, we don't try to jump ahead but instead relish the journey and hope for a satisfying resolution. One moment you're splitting an espresso after class, chuckling over some silly joke about a waiter's mustache. Next thing you know, your fingers are brushing and tangling together, and neither of you can say who reached first. If the vibe's right, you lean in for a kiss—no need for "the talk" or a "So, are we a thing?" speech. It's all there in the way you look at each other, like a secret you both already know. This is the art of mutual seduction, unhampered by social constructs or expectations.

When it comes to romance the French way, the only two rules we have are simple:

1. Keep it casual first; worry about labels later.
2. Don't be afraid to ask personal questions on a first date. The second it gets personal, it gets interesting.

In the spring of 2017, when I was still living in Paris, I asked a girl I liked if she wanted to take a walk. That was it. We ended up walking for forty-five minutes without really knowing our destination. We bought a cheap bottle of wine (I was on a student budget) and found a park with plenty of other couples doing the same thing. We talked for hours about nothing and everything, and I remember my mom calling me, worrying where I was, since suddenly it was 2 a.m. It wasn't supposed to be an all-night thing. But the conversation just kept flowing, and neither of us wanted to stop.

In the U.S., I notice people stick to a script when it comes to love and dating. You go out for dinner, maybe a drink after, and then you both go home. There's this invisible timeline: Don't stay too long, don't text too soon, don't look "too eager."

When I first started dating in the U.S., I went out with a girl I met through a teammate. We grabbed dinner, and I remember sitting there expecting an easy night of talking about random things. Instead, the questions came fast: What's your five-year plan? Do you want kids? What are your "red flags"?

I didn't know how to answer without sounding like I was selling myself. In France, a first date doesn't feel like that. It's more like, let's see if we enjoy this moment together. No one expects you to reveal your life strategy between the appetizer and dessert. I was spending more time thinking about the "right" answer than enjoying her company.

When I finally stopped trying to perform and just told her a funny story about how in my first ever communication class here, I mispronounced beach with b*tch, she laughed so hard she nearly spilled her drink. That was the only time the date felt real.

I learned something important that night: If I bring the same relaxed energy I'd have on a date back home—focusing on connection, not performance—it changes everything. The pressure goes away. The night becomes lighter. And honestly, that's when people actually get to know each other.

Remember that forty-five-minute walk with cheap wine? That walk turned into a weekend, and that weekend turned into a relationship that lasted almost two years. No one was worried about establishing ground rules from the outset. We were just . . . there.

Whenever I tell this story to my American friends, they say, "That would never happen here. You ask a girl to go for a walk with you, and she will call the cops or tell everyone in town you're a stalker." If this is how you'd react, trust me, you are missing out—and not just with me! It's amazing who you can meet in thirty minutes if you give yourself the chance. But you do have to let go of the rules a little and trust the moment to take you where it wants.

NO GAMES (OR RULES) IN LOVE—EXCEPT BE YOURSELF

When we moved to the U.S., Tom and I had a lot to learn about the customs of dating and romance. Casually dating versus officially being a thing. Meticulously planning every date versus going with the flow. But what we realized was that the most important thing was leading with authenticity, approaching people with genuine curiosity and openness, and fostering any potential chemistry with shared humor—in other words, everything the French way is about.

To the French, authenticity is everything. When it comes to romance, there's no need for strategy. If you like someone, show it. If they pop into your mind, send that message. If you want to see them, ask. This whole overthinking every text or playing it cool? Pfff, *c'est ridicule* (ridiculous). Love isn't a chess match—it's about being real.

Tom's budding relationship with his girlfriend Mattie (more on this in a second) made me take a hard look at myself and how I was approaching dating. I'd been coasting on the French accent, charming my way through a thousand first dates—all surface, no roots. I was playing by American rules of dating, but with a French accent that gave me a leg up on the competition. Noncommittal, surface conversations, focused on fun and having a pleasurable time instead of zeroing in on the person across from me and engaging in a way that often feels uncomfortable in the American culture. Here, when you talk to a girl on a first date, if you dive right into her childhood trauma or her views on anything more serious than nail polish, you risk coming off as a creeper or something. So I avoided this in service of a good time. However, it got me nowhere serious.

Then Katherine showed up, with absolutely no patience for my usual tricks. Five minutes into our coffee date, she was grilling me on geopolitics. Ten minutes in, she called me out for hiding behind pretty quotes instead of saying something real. For the first time in forever, I had to show up with more than a smirk. Here was an American girl, treating me like a French girl, while I'm the Frenchie trying to play by her American rules. She very quickly, inadvertently, reminded me of my roots.

What came next was a whirlwind: swapping articles over breakfast, dragging each other to 6 a.m. workouts, and those quiet, fiery arguments that ended in jokes and a playful elbow to the ribs. My French-cad charm I'd leaned on with other American girls was still there, like a dash of *fleur de sel* (finishing salt), but the real flavor came from the substance we were building—together through engaging, sometimes invasive, truth.

Katherine reminded me flirting's a blast, but if there's

nothing solid underneath, the spark fizzles out fast. Love sticks when you drop the act and show up as you—raw, real, no games.

We see our friends in other countries tying themselves in knots over so-called dating rules—waiting hours to text back, acting aloof, crafting vague replies as if they're international spies. But why? What does it achieve? If you pretend to be less interested than you are, how is the other person supposed to know how you feel? That's not intriguing—it's just confusing. Worse, it's self-sabotage.

Every time you delay a response on purpose, every message you leave on read, every carefully calculated silence—you're not winning points; you're building walls. And let's be honest: Love is not a strategy game. It's a connection. So why complicate something that's meant to be simple?

Now, imagine dating the way we do in Paris: Meet someone you like, get excited, find out everything you can about them, and hope for the best. We actually just say what we feel. Shocker, right? That song playing at the store reminds you of them? Tell them. You walk past their favorite pâtisserie? Snap a photo and send it. These little spontaneous moments of connection mean more than any perfectly timed message ever could. Why? Because they're natural and authentic. And natural authenticity beats calculated manipulation or a contrived effort to be aloof every single time.

Being authentic doesn't mean texting nonstop or declaring your undying love on the second date. It just means showing genuine interest and enthusiasm and asking questions that actually let you get to know the person beyond their sense of casual fun.

Too often in America I've heard people say things like, "Oh, it was too much too fast," or, "They were too excited." Like it's a form of weakness or a turnoff for someone to be excited by you. Honestly, since when is enthusiasm a weakness? Isn't someone who has the courage to be open and who is excited about you exactly what you want? It takes real courage to be open, to show you care for someone without knowing if they'll care back. In fact, that's the point: If you're scared off by honesty, you're probably the one playing games. If you're the one who feels like you always put yourself out and get let down when it's not returned, count your blessings. Better to know if the person you are excited about is someone you probably shouldn't be excited about than waste time wondering.

Here's the thing: The best connections are built on trust. When you drop the games, something amazing happens: You make space for real chemistry. You allow for those unplanned, magical moments that happen only when two people are genuinely present with each other. You let someone fall for the real you—not some curated version designed for maximum intrigue.

So drop the walls. Be real. Say what you feel. Ask what you want to know. If they're into it—*fantastique*! If not? At least you were honest, and you can move on with no regrets.

Because in the end, love isn't about winning—it's about showing up as your true self and letting something real happen. And that, *mes amis*, is the French way.

L'histoire de Tom

Waiting Is Just a Waste of Time

When I first met my girlfriend, Mattie, it wasn't some grand, cinematic moment—but to me, it felt like one. We were at one of our first college practices—she was on the women's soccer team; I was on the men's. Same field, different drills. There were a lot of people out there, but to me, she stood out. The way she moved, her focus, her energy—it was impossible not to look at her. And I swear, the few times our eyes met, something clicked.

After practice, although we hadn't spoken, I learned who she was and found her on Instagram. Her profile was full of vibrant photos—her laughing with friends. She just had this bright, positive presence. She was gorgeous. I hit Follow, and to my surprise, she Followed me back almost instantly. That was it for a while, just a quiet digital nod. No messages, just a lot of Likes.

About a week later, I was at a bar playing pool with my buddies, Shane and François. I couldn't stop talking about her—this girl from the soccer team, with her radiant smile and sweet energy. I pulled up her Instagram on my phone, scrolling through her posts like a lovesick teenager.

"Look at her, she's gorgeous," I said, probably for the tenth time. I knew I'd talk to her eventually, but I wasn't scheming or setting a timeline. It was more like a vague "someday" plan, the kind you make when you're too shy to act, especially in a new country, new culture, speaking a new language. So I waited and told myself one day I'd see her at a party and say something.

Then Shane decided to take matters into his own hands. While I was lining up my shot, he grabbed my phone, smirking. I turned just in time to see him click a messaging app link in her bio and add her to my contacts. My heart dropped.

"What are you doing?!" I yelped, snatching the phone back. "She's gonna think I'm some creepy stalker!" Shane just laughed, shrugging like it was no big deal. Now I was stuck—her name was in my app, and I had to say something or look like a weirdo.

The next day, I was getting ready for a house party, one of those big soccer crowd bashes where everyone shows up. I thought she might be there. This was my chance. I opened the app, took a breath, and typed, "Are you going to the party tonight?" I hit send before I could overthink it. She replied right away.

"Yeah, I'll be there:)" I couldn't stop smiling, and I felt a rush—like maybe this wasn't a disaster after all.

At the party, we found each other almost instantly. We talked all night about soccer, life, school, and random stuff that felt important in the moment. It felt natural, easy, like we already knew each other. I hadn't planned anything clever to say, no pickup lines. Just curiosity, honesty, and my broken English. And it worked!

A year or two into our relationship, I told her the story of Shane's pool-table heist. She burst out laughing, then dropped a bombshell.

"You know," she said, her eyes twinkling, "I only added that messaging link to my bio because I was hoping you'd see it. I took it down right after you added me." My jaw dropped. She'd been waiting for me to make a move, too! Shane's boldness saved us both from our own hesitation.

That moment taught me something I'll never forget: Waiting is just a waste of time. Playing it cool, overthinking every text, holding back to seem mysterious—it's all nonsense. I was not letting my French instincts free. I was restraining them.

Sometimes inaction is not letting things develop organically because it is inauthentic. If I wanted to talk to her, I should have done so sooner and without egging on from my pals.

If you like someone, go for it. Be real, be direct, like the French. Don't wait, don't play games. Waiting just means missing moments you could've shared—or worse, building up hope only to find out they're not interested and all that time was for nothing. Honesty and authenticity? They'll give you an answer (and peace of mind).

Taking that first step pushed me out of my fear of upsetting norms, and it led to something real. And honestly, that's how I try to live my life now. No games. Just truth, effort, and a bit of courage. Life's too short to spend it Liking posts instead of living the story.

BEAUTY LIES IN THE MOMENT: THE FIRST DATE

Let's talk about first dates in France because, trust us, they're a whole different vibe. Back home, we don't overthink it. Maybe we meet for an espresso at a cozy little bar, or we share a glass of red at a neighborhood spot we love. If there's chemistry, great. If not, no big deal; we still enjoyed the date.

We've seen how dating works elsewhere, and honestly, it looks exhausting. Fancy dinner reservations, carefully curated outfits, and overanalyzing every little move. The French approach? Simpler. The setting matters, *bien sûr* (of course), but it's more about the ambience than the price tag. We go for places where conversation flows naturally and we can actually hear each other talk. No need for grand gestures—just a relaxed, inviting space where two people can connect and laugh together.

And we have to laugh about something—these activity dates we keep hearing about? Bowling? Escape rooms? Mini golf? *Non, merci*. How are you supposed to have a real conversation while you're trying to solve puzzles or keep track of points? For us, the best dates happen when you're simply sitting across from someone, lost in conversation. It's about swapping stories, sharing passions, and discovering what makes the other person tick, where they've traveled, what they dream about, what excites them. That's the real magic.

But perhaps our favorite thing about dating in France is the lack of rules. There's no checklist of dos and don'ts. Who pays? What do you wear? How long should you wait to text them back? *Franchement* (frankly), who cares? Dating should feel as natural as a walk along the Seine: You let the conversation flow, see where the moment takes you, and enjoy it without overthinking. The moment you start obsessing over the "right" way to do things, you lose the spontaneity that makes dating fun.

At the end of the day, a first date is just that—a first encounter. If it leads to something more, wonderful. If not, at least you shared an interesting conversation over a good drink. And really, what more do you need?

SLOWLY BUT SURELY: THE TIMELINE

So you're being yourself, you meet someone great, and you go on a date with them. You know what else drives us crazy? How so many people we meet are obsessed with checking off certain relationship milestones like they're following some kind of manual. Three dates to kiss, one month to be official, six months to meet the parents—who came up with this stuff?

You know what it looks like to us? People so focused on reaching the next level, they're missing the actual moment they're in. They're on date two but thinking about date five, or they're three months in but stressing about when to move in together. Meanwhile, life—real, beautiful, messy life—is happening right now, and they're not even enjoying it.

Think about those perfect summer nights when you're out with someone new. The conversation's flowing, the music's just right, and time kind of disappears. But instead of sinking into that magic, some people are busy wondering, "What does this mean for next week?" *Arrête*! (Stop!) You're missing everything that truly matters.

Here's what we've learned: Some people open up instantly, like they've known you forever. Others? They're like those stories that reveal themselves chapter by chapter, each page worth waiting for. Both are beautiful. Both are valid. The problem starts when you try to rush to the end of the book instead of enjoying each page.

The relationships Tom and I are currently in both unfolded at their own pace, and allowing them to do so is what has made them strong. Our girlfriends have the same mindset we do. We support each other in every moment, without too much of an eye on the pressures that will come later when things like marriage and children might come into play. Living this way has allowed each of us to succeed in our own ventures in addition to our romantic relationships.

When you stop obsessing over relationship timelines, you start noticing the good stuff. Like how your person brings you your favorite flowers just because, or the way they grab your hand during scary movies, or those random Tuesday nights when you're doing nothing special but somehow it feels perfect.

That's the beauty of staying present. Some days are Instagram-perfect, sure. But the real magic? It's in those messy, unscripted moments: the late-night grocery runs, the failed cooking experiments, the days when you're both kind of grumpy but still want to be around each other.

And here's the thing: When you let go of all these expectations about where you "should" be in your relationship, what grows instead is so much better. It's genuine. It's yours. No comparison to other couples, no checking off boxes, no pressure to hit certain markers by certain dates. Just two people, in the moment, figuring out their own rhythm. Because at the end of the day, that's what makes a relationship worth having—not how fast you got there but how real it feels right now. *C'est la vie.*

I DO

Speaking of timelines: marriage in France? It's not some grand, glittering finish line. In France, it's more of a formality—a legal checkbox rather than the ultimate declaration of love.

Don't get me wrong—the French have long, devoted relationships. There's just no feeling that you have to exchange vows. You might live together for years, raise kids, share a bank account—and still keep your own last name. Instead of a wedding, many opt for a *pacte civil de solidarité*, a legal partnership that grants couples the same rights in terms of taxes, inheritance, and shared assets, minus the pomp and pressure of a ceremony.

Of course, marriage is still respected, but in France, it's not the gold standard of commitment. Love isn't something you prove with paperwork—it's something you live. A couple can be wildly in love and see no reason to "make it official." It's more about being together than checking off milestones.

So no, romance and marriage don't always go hand in hand. Romance is about passion, shared moments, and deep connection. Marriage? It's just paperwork. A practical decision, not a prerequisite for love.

That said, if marriage is your dream, by all means, have the wedding of your dreams. Just don't let it define what love should look like. The real magic? It's in the journey—not the contract.

LIVE AND LET LIVE: YOU ARE STILL YOU

There's often this cultural emphasis in the U.S. on "becoming one" once you commit to a relationship—merging your friend groups, hobbies, and even social media accounts to create this perfect couple dynamic. And while that works for some, we Frenchies believe there's a different way.

For us, it's all about maintaining our individuality—even in the closest relationships. We don't need matching outfits or shared accounts to prove we're in love. We celebrate the little things that make each of us unique, even while we're together. If there's one thing the French cherish, it's freedom—within love and beyond.

Before you break up with us, don't get us wrong—we're totally about love and commitment. But having your own life? That's essential. Whether you're twenty-five, forty-five, sixty-five, or eighty-five, doing your own thing is just as important as the romantic stuff. When our partners are out having fun with their friends, we're not sitting at home checking their location or spiraling with worry. We're out living our own lives, seeing our own friends, doing our own things. And you know what? That's exactly how it should be.

The cool thing about relationships where partners give adequate space to one another? Everyone keeps their own identity. Sure, we share amazing moments together, but we don't turn into this weird two-headed creature where we can't make a single move without consulting each other. We've all got our own interests. Maybe one of us loves playing sports with friends while the other is into art galleries and yoga. We don't need to do everything together. It's about giving each other room to grow while still being crazy about each other. That's the sweet spot.

And those times apart? They just make us appreciate each other more. Trust us, nothing keeps the spark alive like having stories to share when you come back together.

L'histoire de Tom

Balancing Me Versus Us

My girlfriend and I have a relationship that thrives on freedom, not fusion. Don't get me wrong—I love when we're together. But I'm not the kind of boyfriend who thinks we need to be glued at the hip. I cherish her independence as much as I do my own, and that's what keeps our connection strong.

Take my work, for example. It keeps me busy, often pulling me out of New Orleans for days or weeks, or even just locking me in my home office for hours. I travel, I hustle, and I can't expect Mattie to just wait around for me. Some weeks, I'm barely home, so she needs her friends, her nights out, her own rhythm to keep her happy. And I want that for her.

I've seen what happens when couples don't make room for independence. Some lose themselves in the relationship so much that they forget how to be their own person. No hobbies outside each other, no separate plans, no alone time. And eventually, they get tired, bored, even resentful. What starts as closeness slowly turns into suffocation.

I've never wanted that for me, or for us. I want my girlfriend to have her girls' nights, to laugh and connect in ways that are different from ours. Sometimes, I'm the one nudging her. "Baby, you haven't seen Juliet in a week—text her, go hang out," I'll say. And she'll light up, grab her phone, and make it happen. Meanwhile, I've got my own crew—my brother, my buddies, the guys I grab beers with. We've all got our own lives, our own stories, and that's what keeps things fresh when we come back together.

At the same time, we have passions we share that make us even stronger. For example, we love playing soccer together every Tuesday and Sunday. It's a way to reconnect with how we met, but also to be more than just girlfriend and boyfriend. We're teammates for an hour, making each other score, laugh, and play with our friends.

On the field we make our own choices, and at home we do, too: I might want to watch a TV show or work on my DJ skills, while she prefers to read a book or just take time for herself. That balance keeps things healthy and fun.

And then, when it comes to daily life, we divide and conquer. If she loads the dishwasher, I unload it; if I cook, she cleans the dishes; if she wipes the countertops, I vacuum. We find ways to make life smoother together while still keeping our individuality. And it's in those little things that we remind ourselves we're building something side by side. This chapter talks about *chacun son chemin*—to each their own path, and we often find ourselves together many times along the way, which makes it even better, and that's our vibe.

Sometimes, she'll have a girls' night but invite me along. "I want you there," she'll say, and I'm happy to join because I'm friends with her crew, and some of their boyfriends are my buddies, too. It's natural, not forced. We hang out, laugh, and it feels like a big, messy family. Other times, she wants it to be just the girls, and I'm all for it. "Go have fun," I tell her, and I mean it. If she wants me there, I'm there. If she doesn't, I'm just as happy chilling at home or out with my own friends. Whatever makes her light up works for me.

When we're not in the same place, we don't blow up each other's phones; we trust each other enough to give space. For example, when I spend the whole day filming with Alex, I'll let her know I won't be answering for a few hours and check in once I'm done. Or if I'm out at the bar with my friends, I tell her I probably won't be on my phone much. She does the same with me: She'll send me a quick video of her dancing with her friends or playing games, and I know it's her time to enjoy. I don't need to text her every five minutes. When you give each other freedom, you're not just respecting space—you're building a relationship that feels alive and secure. You're not together because you *have* to be—you're together because you *want* to be. Like the chapter says, love isn't about control; it's about showing up authentically and letting the other person do the same.

When we're apart, it makes coming back together sweeter. After a girls' night, she'll crash onto the couch with me, giggling about some story from her friends, and say, "I missed you." Or I'll come back from playing pool with the guys still buzzing from a good game, and realize I can't wait to see her. We'll plan a dinner date not because it's scheduled but because we genuinely want to be together. As the French say, "Se manquer, c'est se retrouver plus fort." Missing each other makes reuniting even stronger.

We also love traveling the world together, and just like in our daily lives, we apply the same balance. Going on road trips with your partner is such a revealing way to understand their personality and what they need. We always have a rough plan when we travel, but we never schedule every single minute. Leaving room for spontaneity, whether it's a random detour to a hidden café or deciding to chase a sunset, lets us see each other's true selves and keeps the adventure alive. It's in those unscripted moments that we learn to trust each other and respect each other's space, needs, and wants. One day in the South of France, we decided to spend the whole day in Spain instead, just because why not, and that's exactly what makes a trip magical.

This very French way of being in a relationship is simple: Let your partner do what makes them happy. If they want you along, jump in. If they want to fly solo, cheer them on. Trust them to live their life and trust yourself to live yours. At the end of the day, if they want to be with you, they will. And that kind of love just feels natural and cozy, like home. And somehow, no matter what, our mornings or evenings always end up with our cat, Bambi, snuggling right in between the two of us.

THE ART OF EVERYDAY ROMANCE: MEANINGFUL GESTURES

The French have long been the masters of romance, but let's set the record straight—it's not because we're constantly planning grand gestures or pulling off cinematic love stories. *Non, non*. Real romance isn't about sweeping someone off their feet. It's about keeping them floating, effortlessly, every single day. While other cultures might save romance for anniversaries, Valentine's Day, or big declarations, we understand that love thrives in the *glimmers*—the small, consistent moments that keep the spark alive, every single day.

I remember one time I opened my door to find, on the handle, a tiny bundle of *muguet* (lily of the valley) from my girlfriend at the time and a note wishing me luck on my exam. In France, we give *muguet* on May 1 for good luck. It's simple and cheap, but it's a warm gesture. I put it in a glass on my desk. I also loved that it broke the stereotype. This time a girl gave flowers to a guy!

The most meaningful gestures? They often don't cost a *centime* (cent). It's knowing exactly how your person takes their morning coffee or tea and having it ready before they even ask. It's sending a quick message when you pass the place where you first met. It's hiding a loving note in their pocket just because. These small acts speak louder than any grand declaration because they show you're paying attention—that they're on your mind even in the middle of your busiest day.

True romance lives in those in-between moments, the little rituals you create together. The kiss goodbye before running out the door. That unspoken agreement to always save them the last bite of dessert. A lazy Sunday morning watching your shared favorite show. These small traditions become a shared language, a secret rhythm only the two of you understand.

And let's not forget *ces petits gestes* (small gestures)—the light touch on their back as you move through a crowded café, the way your fingers absentmindedly find their hair during a movie, the effortless intertwining of hands while picking out fresh produce at the market.

Romance isn't reserved for the early stages of dating either—it's a continuous dance of intrigue, teasing, and attraction. The French believe that those subtle gestures, flirtation, and appreciation are what keep the spark alive.

In the end, real romance, the French way, isn't about turning heads. It's about turning toward a person and making them feel truly seen.

REFINED AFFECTION: KISSES AND PDA

Speaking of turning toward someone, when it comes to public displays of affection, the French are romantic—but not *obnoxious*. There's a distinct difference between intimacy and exhibitionism, and most French couples know where the line is—and how to dance right up to it without doing the emotional equivalent of grinding in the canned goods aisle at Whole Foods.

In France, affection is subtle, chic, and suggestive. A gentle touch on the lower back, a lingering look, a quick kiss that says, "I missed you," not, "I'm trying to inhale your face." You might see a couple holding hands while walking, sharing a book at the park, or whispering something flirty during a long lunch. But you won't often catch them straddling each other on a bench or making out like it's the final scene of a teen drama.

Contrast that with the other places we've traveled to, where PDA (public display of affection) is often either *nonexistent* (think couples sitting next to each other like tax auditors at a diner) or . . . aggressively everywhere. We've witnessed full-blown make-out sessions in grocery store parking lots and couples practically dry-humping each other in the airport security line. There's a kind of go-big-or-go-home energy to American PDA. It's not that Americans are more passionate—it's that there's less of a filter, less of that French sense of "mystery is sexy."

To us, the most romantic gestures are the ones that hint, not scream. The French approach to PDA is like a good perfume: You notice it when you lean in, not when it chokes the whole elevator. It's knowing when to pull someone in close and when to simply lock eyes across the room and smile. It's about connection, not performance. Americans might call it restrained. We call it refined.

What's also different is how we *talk* about love in public. French couples tend to keep declarations private. We don't need a social media slideshow or an anniversary post longer than a dissertation to prove we're in love. The proof is, as I mentioned, in the small things: the way someone orders your coffee just the way you like it, or how they touch your hand midconversation. Love isn't a status update—it's a feeling.

Of course, times are changing, and even some French couples are getting bolder with their affections thanks to global culture and social media's demand for kissing selfies. But at our core, we still believe that a little restraint makes the affection mean more.

Let the intimacy stay between you two—at least until

you're home. Or at the very least until you're not blocking a Starbucks exit.

Leave it to two Frenchies to have to revert to their French ways to find love with two American girls. And let this be a lesson to us all: The kind of love that has the potential to feel real can come only from being as real as we can be with each other. Don't show up to a first, second, or third date wearing a mask (unless you're both into that sort of thing). Just show up. Show up without expectation but with curiosity. Show up without insecurity but with confidence. Show up with *your* sense of humor; don't try to borrow one. Shared laughter, when it's genuine, doesn't just break the ice; it melts it completely. A forced smile, likewise, can suck the warmth out of an entire evening.

Finding a spark with the potential to grow into a flame really starts with being yourself, no matter the consequence. Be okay with who you are regardless of who the other person turns out to be. Don't concern yourself with whether or not they will be into you, even if you *are* into them! Not everyone is a good match. Not every date will go the way you hope. Don't feel bad if finding that genuine connection seems to be difficult. It is difficult, but it will only be more difficult to find real connection if you aren't really who you present yourself to be.

Chapter 6.

SAVOR EVERY BITE

Avec Tom

Close your eyes for a second and picture the madness of a morning gone to hell: Cereal careens across the counter, tumbling like a waterfall down the side of your kitchen island. There's a deadline clawing at your nerves. You just realized the milk splattered your shirt, so now you have to change and there's already a line of ants marching toward the lost Fruit Loops. The day is unraveling before it's even kicked off. You're already drowning in the rush, shackled to the clock's merciless tick.

Now ditch that. Imagine instead a cobblestone street in Paris, tucked away from the noise, where a little café buzzes with quiet defiance of rush. The chairs are worn but solid, the waiter drifts by with a shrug, and there, in front of you, a softly boiled egg is cradled in its shell, yolk golden and trembling, a sunrise waiting to be broken, like it hit the snooze button one last time. Warm, golden pastry hugged by light, flaky goodness. Espresso swirls up in dark, fragrant wisps, slicing through the fog of your thoughts. Sometimes a little yogurt or piece of fruit sneaks in, but that's about as wild as it gets.

This isn't just a meal—it's a middle finger to the storm, a stolen breath, a heartbeat slowed to the now.

Snap back to reality, to the American breakfast dream, a towering fortress of excess—pancakes stacked like skyscrapers, eggs scrambled into submission, bacon sizzling in greasy glory, maybe even topped with a bold dollop of melted cheese. It's a show, a circus on a plate, and you dive in, fork flying, because that's the drill—consume, conquer, move on. But stop and think: Can you taste it? Really taste it? The flavors crash like a riot, a firehose blasting your senses till they buckle. It's everything at once, and yet it's nothing—each bite lost in the chaos, a blur of chewing and heat that leaves you stuffed but hollow.

This chapter isn't just about food (though we'll talk about it plenty). It's about learning that meals aren't just background noise. They aren't an inconvenience on your way to do something important. They teach you to slow down, to notice, and to connect.

Whether it's duck confit or the best bowl of ramen you've ever had, savoring a meal is about giving the act of consuming meaning. That's the French way. It's what Alex and I grew up with, and that's what we want you to carry with you every time you sit down at a table: an appreciation for the most fundamental ritual we humans have.

FOOD REQUIRES THAT YOU PAY ATTENTION

My mom always made family meals a big deal. Cooking is how she shows her love—I swear you can taste the love she pours into every bite. Her Caesar salad (her homemade dressing was just unreal). Her butternut squash and coconut curry soup (she could make anyone love butternut with that one). Her special salad with avocado, mango, shrimp, bacon, and secret sauce (hands down my favorite salad ever). Honestly, if my mom ever wrote a cookbook, it would become a bestseller.

Growing up, my brother and I never winced at the colors or textures of our meals because we were raised to appreciate cuisine. That's the way French parents operate. While kids in other places are stuck with the same old neon-orange mac and cheese and chicken nuggets, we French kids eat whatever our parents eat: nibbling on a baguette still warm from the *boulangerie* (bakery) or twirling forkfuls of garlicky escargots (okay, that's an exaggeration—not everyone in France eats snails, but you get the idea!). My *maman* didn't even blink when she slid a bowl of *blanquette de veau* (a French veal stew) my way when I was just a kid, broth dripping with wine and parsley, daring me to dive in. And dive I did.

In France, trying new foods is not a chore but a pleasure. An education. An education in pleasure. By the time we're grown, that early baptism in flavor turns us into adults who can taste the difference between a tomato kissed by the sun and one gassed into submission. We don't just eat—we judge, we savor, we revel. That's why, as a twentysomething tearing through Paris, I'd rather save my euros for one perfect ham and cheese than waste them on a pile of mediocre takeout.

Learning to taste isn't just about flavor; it's about expertise. It's about sharpening your awareness toward food and the nuance in a dish. My brother and I were trained to notice when the vinaigrette had too much mustard or when the ratatouille lacked thyme. My mom would even turn it into a game: We had to guess exactly which ingredients were in the soup, the salad, the dessert—whatever we were eating. The closer we got to the real recipe, the more she beamed.

Food doesn't have to be fancy or French to be meaningful. It just needs your full attention. And when you think about it, that kind of attention doesn't just stay on the plate but spills into everything. The French palate becomes the French mindset: charming, precise, and unapologetically opinionated.

SAVOR THE MOMENT AS MUCH AS THE MEAL

In France, you rarely eat alone. Even at work, there will always be a baguette passed around the lunch table and a dozen conversations bouncing between sports, the latest news, and weekend plans. No eating in silence at your desk while watching a show. Meals have their own rhythm, and if you eat too fast, you miss the point.

In the U.S., it's different. When we were in college, we'd see our classmates not schedule time between classes for lunch. They would simply grab and go, shoveling a tuna wrap into their mouths on their way to class, or worse, in the desk next to me midlecture.

My dad, the unofficial food speed police, used to scold us for rushing. As a kid, I didn't get it. I just wanted to finish and go play. Now, I understand: Food and family are one. The table is where the deepest debates happen, where core memories are made, where presence matters.

Take a classic *soupe à l'oignon*, for example—deep golden broth, onions cooked down until they're soft and sweet, with cheese just starting to melt into the top. That's not something you rush through. You take your time with it, spoon after spoon, letting it warm you up from the inside. Add your best friends, a bottle of wine, a wobbly old table, and some stories flying across it, and suddenly it's not just dinner; it's connection. Those shared meals tie us together, keeping loneliness from creeping in.

PLEASURE WITHOUT GUILT

But beyond all that, food is about pleasure without guilt. A perfect croissant that shatters just right when you bite into it . . . *miam*! (yum!) That alone can make a gray Monday feel like the best day.

Butter isn't the enemy—and neither is sugar, wine, or carbs. What matters is balance, and joy. We eat slowly, stop when we're almost full, and say yes to dessert when we want to. The real excess is not on the plate; it's in the rush, the guilt, and the self-judgment. In France, the pleasure of eating is part of health, not a threat to it.

While on a date in New Orleans, my girlfriend, Mattie, and I shared four scoops of ice cream from a famous shop. For a moment, the rest of the world faded away. No rush, no guilt, no "we shouldn't have"—just pure joy. Each flavor was its own little surprise, and we enjoyed every bite. But more than the taste, it was about the simple happiness of being together, and the quiet magic of turning something as small as ice cream into a memory that sticks.

QUALITY OVER QUANTITY

We French see it differently, and *mon Dieu*, it burns in our souls to tell you this: It's not about the mountain of food—it's about that one radiant spark of perfection.

Picture one pancake—not a stack, not a pile, just one. A pancake so flawless, so damn well-made, its golden edge crisp yet soft, its taste a melody of the perfectly crafted cinnamon compound butter, the faint sweetness of caramelized fresh apple, topped with a dollop of house-made whipped cream. That is worth more than that whole American sprawl. You don't shovel it down in a thirty-minute sprint, treating it like gas for your daily grind, each bite a competition to see how much you can fit in your mouth. *Non*, you linger. You take bites as small as possible to deliver the flavor and extend the experience. Thirty minutes stretch into a holy ritual, each bite a meditation, each second a shout: I'm here, I'm alive, and this—*this*—is worth it.

Quality over quantity is our gospel, carved deep into the bones of French living. Food just to fill you up? It's a dead weight dragging your spirit down. But food as pleasure, as a dance for your senses? It lifts you, holds you, sets you on fire with possibility. Fewer ingredients, *oui*—but each one a star, picked with care, savored with respect. A perfect peach from the farm stand, its juice a burst of summer. A hunk of bread, crust cracking like a song, its core soft and giving. Compare that to the avalanche of meh—piles of bland, lifeless grub that leave you heavier in body but lighter in soul.

This isn't snobbery—it's freedom. It's a battle cry against the tyranny of too much, a plea to take back your mornings, your days, your life. Start with quality, let it sink into your bones, and watch it reshape everything. That croissant isn't just a pastry—it's a manifesto. That pancake isn't just breakfast—it's a revolution. Choose less, choose better, and feel the ground shift under you.

L'histoire d'Alex

My First Time Giving Thanks

Let me tell you about my first Thanksgiving. Thanksgiving, for the uninitiated, is an American holiday in late November where families roast a turkey the size of a small scooter, bake pies in every flavor known to humankind, and give thanks for, well, mostly the food.

My very first Thanksgiving in the U.S. happened in Diamondhead, Mississippi, with one of Tom's friends and her family. And let me tell you, for a French person like me, it was . . . an experience. I flew in from Ohio to Mississippi for a full week, and the moment I landed, I knew my first Southern Thanksgiving would be epic.

I remember being stunned by the food. I sat there in front of my empty plate, not knowing where to start. In France, a "big dinner" is four courses, five if someone is feeling ambitious. In Mississippi? I think there were fifteen dishes on the table. Minimum. So many casseroles with ingredients I still cannot identify. Pies made out of vegetables . . . but also sugar? There was a smoked turkey *and* a fried turkey. And then the infamous *turducken*, the Frankenstein of poultry. I didn't know whether to eat it or file a report.

For me, the whole spread felt a bit strange, but I tried everything. And I liked most of it. Best of all was the cozy vibe of the holiday. The hospitality was immediate and real. I arrived, and within ten minutes I had been hugged, fed, and called "sweetheart." One woman told me, "You're family now." In France, we don't even say that to our *actual* family sometimes.

Then I learned the real tradition comes after the feast: Everyone slides into a collective food coma, sprawls on the couch, and watches American football until consciousness returns. I wasn't shocked in a bad way—it was more like cultural whiplash. The sheer joy of eating until you can't move! But also . . . you literally can't move. The French *sieste* is delicate. The Thanksgiving nap is an extreme sport.

At seventeen, I didn't question any of this abundance. I just went along with it. Burgers, fries, giant sodas—it was exciting, this American generosity! I remember my first McDonald's run in Ohio. I ordered what I thought was a "medium" soda, and the cashier handed me a plastic bucket that could double as a flower vase. In France, that thing is a *grand*—our biggest size. (And yes, McDo—our affectionate nickname for McDonald's—is wildly popular back home, and believe it or not, it's way better and healthier.)

Here, every meal felt like a mission to feel *full*—not just content, but that heavy, almost uncomfortable fullness that makes you want to nap. After a couple of years, I noticed that mindset creeping into my eating habits. I'd finish a massive plate and think, "Okay, now I'm done," not because I was really done but because I couldn't fit another bite. It was like my brain forgot how to eat for pleasure and started eating to conquer.

When I went back to France for summer or Christmas breaks, I'd sit at my parents' table and complain that the portions were too small! I was craving that overstuffed feeling. But here's the French secret: Give it an hour or two, and your body catches up. Your stomach settles, your brain registers the meal, and you feel satiated, not like you've swallowed a bowling ball. The French don't chase that "I can't eat another bite" moment. It's not about *je ne peux plus* (I can't anymore); it's about *je n'ai plus besoin* (I don't need more). That's why French bodies are often so healthy—not from deprivation but from mindfulness, from eating with intention.

My dad, *mon héros* in so many ways, saw this American ogre—*oui, ogre*—taking over his son and stepped in. He's always been my guide, especially with food. During those breaks, he'd watch me shovel down meals like I hadn't eaten in weeks and say, "*Doucement, mon fils*. Slow down. Food is not a race." He'd remind me to take my time, to chew, to taste, to let the meal be an *expérience*.

"You don't eat to be full," he'd say. "You eat to enjoy, to feel good in your body." No food babies, no nausea, just pleasure. I'd roll my eyes, but deep down, I knew he was right.

I saw it in my body, too—those extra pounds from rushing through meals, from forgetting why we eat in the first place.

That French approach to dining, I almost lost it in those early U.S. years. But by twenty, I started relearning my French roots. I'd pause between bites, savor the flavors on my *palais* (palate), and stop when I felt good, not when my plate was empty. Eating became less about filling a void and more about celebrating the moment—the crunch of a fresh radish, the warmth of a homemade soup.

Now, bouncing between the U.S. and France, I'm still finding my balance. In Los Angeles, I sometimes slip back into the American way—big plates, quick meals—because it's all around me. But when I'm in France, surrounded by my family, I fall back into that French rhythm: smaller portions, slower bites, conversations that stretch past dessert. I don't want to look like I'm starving when I sit at a French table, *non, merci*! It's a dance, this back-and-forth, and I'm still learning the steps.

My dad's voice echoes: "Look at what's on your plate, not how much, but what. Know the story behind it." Even if it's not a Michelin-star meal—and let's be honest, most nights it's not—understanding your food, its flavors, its origins, makes every bite richer.

You don't just eat to be full; you eat to feel alive.

FRENCHIFY YOUR FOOD GAME

You don't need a beret or a fancy *R* roll to work a kitchen like a true Frenchie. The rules of French dining are simpler, grounded—a little uprising you can stir up in your own pot.

But first, ditch the delivery app. Forget massive casseroles and twenty-course meals—dining à la française is about small plates packed with soul and popping with taste. And you don't need a brick of a recipe book, just a few fresh picks and a little love.

Okay, ready? Let's dive into what makes French eating feel like *living*.

Choose Quality Ingredients

First up: produce. The grocery aisles in the States can feel like a bit of a letdown sometimes. You've got apples with that glossy, waxy finish, looking promising but tasting kinda meh, as if they forgot the flavor on the way. Green beans sit there, a little droopy, missing that fresh snap after too long in transit. Carrots are all lined up, perfectly orange and identical, built more for shelf life than for popping with taste. You take a bite, and it's just . . . a faint, watery whisper, slipping by without much to say.

It's easy to see why many of our American friends reach for the BBQ or cheese sauce to jazz things up—you're not really savoring. You're just making it work.

Over in France, we don't settle for less. Our veggies aren't just sidekicks—they're the main event, each bringing its own flair. Green beans hit you with a fresh, crisp pop, full of life. Asparagus comes in with that bold, grassy bite. Peas deliver sweet little pops. Zucchini keeps it mellow and smooth. They're not carbon copies—each one's got its own groove on your taste buds.

If every veggie turns into the same bland mush, how do you figure out what you actually like? You might just think, "Eh, veggies aren't for me," when really, you haven't met the real ones yet.

You deserve better. Strawberries that are red all the way through, juicy and real. Tomatoes warm from the sun, bursting with tang. Carrots that crunch with a hint of sweetness, spinach with a deep kick, radishes that wake you up with a peppery zap—eating these isn't a chore; it's an eye-opener.

We're not saying flavorful vegetables are a French thing—not at all. We're saying mass-produced produce that came from a conveyor belt simply isn't the way.

Check out a farmers' market where you can smell the earth in the air, or a roadside stand where everything still feels fresh from the ground. Mass-produced stuff can feel like a factory shortcut—picked early, ripened artificially, shipped forever. But the good stuff? It's grown close by, handled gently, and left to ripen naturally.

Don't have regular access to local farmers or can't suss out what is or is not fresh? Aim for seasonality. Learn what is or is not in season. Your favorites not in season? Don't settle for watered-down versions of what you normally go for and instead try something new. You never know what flavor, texture, or aroma you might discover by chasing freshness over familiarity. Buy in season, and say goodbye to soggy, flavorless veggies.

It's not about being fancy—it's about not missing out. Quality ingredients don't just keep you going; they wake you up. Turn a bite into something you remember, a meal into a moment. Life's too short for dull flavors—go for the real, the vibrant, the stuff that counts.

Try at Least One Bite

I don't think French people are braver with food—we're just nosy. We poke everything with a fork. At home, my parents had one rule: Take one bite, *then* you can say no. It made trying stuff feel normal, not a big identity thing.

In the U.S., I've met super-nice people who don't cross certain lines with food: no fish, no mushrooms, weird textures. They just don't like it. It's not closed-minded; it's comfort—and America is elite at comfort.

But there's so much you miss out on when you prioritize comfort over flavor. A good friend here once told me, "I don't do mushrooms." So we made them two ways: shaved thin with lemon and Parmesan (fresh and crunchy) and seared hard in butter with garlic (deep and nutty). He didn't become a mushroom guy necessarily, but he saw that "mushroom" isn't just one thing.

It goes both ways. Eventually, I had to admit that the

U.S. sauce game is legit. Ranch with veggies? Delicious! Basically our herby yogurt. Buffalo wings? I actually love the spice now. I went from being careful to fully embracing the heat, and now I'm on a mission to make Alex love it too . . . even though he still treats spicy food like punishment. And the classic 2 a.m. snack? A peanut butter and jelly sandwich, obviously. Add a fancy vanilla-bean milkshake or a Nutella chocolate shake, and I'm in heaven. See? Cultural shock goes both ways; sometimes you resist, sometimes you fall in love.

For the French, curiosity at the table is a form of politeness. You taste what's on your plate so you can talk about it, understand it, and experience it. And if you still don't like it, no drama; you don't have to finish it. So if I had to give gentle advice to picky eaters, it would be this: Start small, stay curious, and make it fun. Try the one-bite rule. Keep a "safety flavor" you already love nearby (lemon, butter, BBQ, soy sauce, ranch), something familiar to bridge the gap. If texture is the problem, change it. Raw and thin versus crispy and golden are two completely different worlds. Start mild: cod before salmon, anchovy in a dressing before a whole fillet. Keep portions tiny so the risk feels low.

Try new foods when you're actually hungry. Cook it yourself or watch someone do it. Once you see garlic sizzling in butter, a squeeze of lemon hitting the pan, and herbs being tossed in at the last second, everything suddenly feels simple instead of scary. Food becomes curiosity, not fear.

Try these (trust me): Fish tacos with cod, cabbage, and

lime. Baked white fish with lemon and crispy breadcrumbs. Mushrooms raw with lemon and Parmesan, or pan-fried hard with thyme until golden. Tinned fish mashed with a little mayo and mustard from Dijon on toast. Vegetables roasted hot until they're sweet and caramelized. Strong cheeses melted—like a grilled cheese with a drizzle of honey or a few apple slices.

Because the worst thing that can happen is you don't like it. But the best? You discover a new favorite, a new habit, maybe even a new way to look at the world.

Serve Your Meal in Courses

You know how restaurants serve food in courses? First an appetizer, maybe a salad, then the main dish, and finally dessert. We noticed that in a lot of American homes, the opposite happens: We pile everything onto the table and then onto our plates at once. We consume everything, but not in unison. Meals are as short as possible. Once again, pacing and time are thrown out the window before we ever sit down to enjoy the fruits of either.

A typical French meal follows a structure, not out of formality but out of reverence. Less is more—but it's also better. Instead of presenting and consuming everything at once, our kitchen serves as the backstage area for the dining room. There, we assemble all the elements of the meal and bring out each dish one at a time.

We begin with a simple starter: maybe a soup, a green salad, or a side of roasted veggies. We follow that with a main: chicken with potatoes, a filet of fish with lentils, or a seasonal vegetable tart. If we're feeling extra, we add a cheese course (always served at room temperature with good bread) and end with dessert: dark chocolate, a fruit tart, or just a dish of ripe strawberries with a dollop of cream. No need to be fancy. We just make each course count.

This isn't just better for appreciating the food. It's better for appreciating the company as well. How can you possibly have substantive conversation if you are rushing through your meal? French meals are social by nature. We talk, we argue, we connect—because we have the time to. Small talk is fine, but surface-level chatter won't carry you through a proper French dinner. Ask real questions. Share opinions. Debate ideas. The goal isn't politeness—it's presence. No phones, no distractions. Just people, good food, and conversation that might zigzag from politics to philosophy to why that particular cheese tastes better today than yesterday.

This carries on after the final course as well. There's a moment reserved for the digestif—an after-dinner drink. It doesn't have to be alcoholic, but it frequently is. This is the moment where we let the meal settle, but it's also an opportunity to wrap up those conversations. This is the *dénouement* (outcome) of any great meal and possibly the most important phase. It's a chance to sit back and appreciate what was just built and experienced. Savor a job well done.

So, don't jump up when the meal ends. Plan to linger. Pour another glass. Let the conversation wander and the night stretch long past dessert. This is where the real magic happens. The digestion of ideas, the laughter, the connection. Let the dishes pile up for a minute. Let yourself be full—not just from food but from the moment.

Remember the Etiquette

There's a lot of etiquette when it comes to dining the French way. Even bread has its etiquette in France: You don't cut bread—you break it with your hands. Afterward, it lives on the tablecloth, not your plate. And you don't munch on it mindlessly before the meal starts. Bread is a tool. It's for sauce-sopping, cheese-carrying, and pleasure-enhancing. And yes, it is served with almost everything. But it's not a snack—it's part of the ritual.

Don't overthink attire. Effortlessness is a virtue. Casual elegance is the goal with the food as well as the feel of your clothes. We don't dress for dinner as if we're headed to a ball, but we do care. Clean jeans, a crisp shirt, brushed hair—it's about showing up with intention, not perfection. The same goes for the food: It doesn't have to be complex, but it should feel considered. Plate it nicely. Let the presentation greet their eyes before the scent has a chance to reach their nose, or the taste to reach their lips.

If you're a guest in a Frenchified home, remember the unspoken rules: Don't arrive early. Bring a small, thoughtful gift—a bottle of wine, a bar of good chocolate, a bouquet of flowers. Compliment the food, even if the chicken is dry or the tart is burnt. The host's effort matters. So does the grace of the guest.

Set the Mood

The ambience of a meal isn't just some extra touch—it's what turns the whole thing into an experience that makes it worth it. A meal, no matter how simple, is transformed by its setting. In France, even a frozen quiche tastes better with real plates and soft lighting.

The table is an essential part of the experience. So set up a dining table—scratched up or shiny, it doesn't matter. Just make it a spot. Use a carafe of water, not a plastic bottle. Set out a basket of bread. Crack a window so the breeze can do its thing. We were raised to set the tone for a proper meal—so no TV blaring, no laptop glare as you hunch like a gremlin. Don't have any sounds that interfere with your thoughts. Play some inspiring music instead, something relaxing that feels good. No screens!

Then, light a candle—even on a Tuesday. A little mood lighting goes a long way. Nothing fancy if you don't have it—just a well-placed lamp with a soft amber bulb. But for the love of all things holy, step away from the overhead kitchen lighting. You're not performing surgery—you're having dinner.

Do these things, and *boom*! You're not just eating—you're *in* it. Living a memory as you make it. You're not zoning out while delivering fork to mouth (that's how you turn a good bite into a ghost).

You don't have to do this only when dining at home either. When you're out and about, skip the car crumbs and desk slouch. Instead, grab a blanket, hit a park, and plop under a tree or on a bench with a view worth taking in. This is you telling the world, "Yeah, this meal's got my attention." Eating in a rush while sitting on the hood of your car or staring at spreadsheets? It just keeps you stuck in the same old cycle. Step off and take a pause. You deserve it. Life's too packed with chaos to let meals fade into it.

Don't Finish Prematurely

Next up: dessert. Dessert is not just some sugar bomb tacked on to fill a gap. It's a legit part of the meal, treated with respect but not overblown hype. The French don't see it as this guilty splurge you've got to whisper apologies for. It's more like a smooth closer, a little reward that rounds things out without hijacking the whole show.

As you now know, when it comes to food the French way, we are big on quality over quantity. So portion-wise, dessert should be minimal—think a sliver, not a towering slab of cake that leaves you in a coma. It should also have character—fresh fruit, buttery pastry, maybe a hit of dark chocolate—stuff that tastes like it came from the earth, not a factory. It's not about drowning you in sweetness—it's a tease of flavor that lingers, like the last note of a good song.

Take a classic French dessert like *mousse au chocolat*. It's silky and rich, but you're not spooning it out of a bucket. Or a *clafoutis* with cherries that pop against a custardy base—simple, but it slaps. Even at home, it's less "Let's bake a three-layer beast" and more "Here's a yogurt with honey or a piece of fruit that's actually ripe."

Culturally, dessert is woven into the rhythm of dining; dinner's not done until that sweet note hits, but it's no big drama. Kids grow up eating dessert, so it's not this rare treat you hoard—it's just how meals roll. Dining out, you might see a fromage course before or instead of dessert, but if dessert's on deck, it's still that refined little flex—elegant, not excessive. We're not sweating calories or preaching deprivation. We just figure a bite of something real beats a pile of fake any day. It's less "dessert as sin" and more "dessert as the encore"—a classy wink to wrap dinner up right.

One of our favorite desserts is *galette des rois*, made of golden, flaky puff pastry discs, sandwiching a velvety filling of almond powder, sweet sugar, and butter—so soft it's practically whispering *je t'aime*. A couple of eggs whip it into creamy perfection, and voilà—pure decadence.

Traditionally, the French hide a *fève* (a tiny trinket) inside, and whoever finds it? Instant royalty, crowned with a paper crown and major bragging rights. Serve it warm, sip some cider or bubbly, and indulge in the delicious galette.

French King Cake

(GALETTE DES ROIS)

Ingredients (for 6–8 servings)

2 puff pastry sheets
100 g (½ cup) sugar
75 g (⅓ cup) softened butter
140 g (1⅓ cups) almond powder (ground almonds)
3 eggs (2 whole eggs for the filling, 1 egg yolk for brushing)

Instructions

1. Preheat the oven to 200°C (400°F, thermostat 6–7). Place one puff pastry sheet in a pie dish and prick it with a fork.
2. In a bowl, mix the almond powder, sugar, 2 whole eggs, and softened butter until smooth.
3. Spread the almond filling evenly over the pastry in the dish.
4. Cover with the second puff pastry sheet, pressing the edges firmly to seal.

5. Score decorative patterns on the top with a knife and brush with the egg yolk for a golden finish.

6. Bake for 20–30 minutes, checking regularly until golden and crisp.

Enjoy your galette des rois!

Walk It Off

A meal's magic doesn't simply fade when you stack the plates, especially in a spot like Paris, where the whole setup plays into it. In Paris, driving's not the default; the city's built for your feet. You finish a killer dinner at a friend's place, and instead of piling into a car, you lace up and stroll home. Same deal after a restaurant. Once you're done, you're out the door, stepping into the night.

Those ten to thirty minutes of walking aren't just logistics; they're a low-key superpower. Your stomach gets a gentle nudge to sort itself out, with no bloat or heaviness slowing you down, and your head gets a breather—time to mull over the laughs, the drinks, or just the cobblestones under your soles.

Compare that to the States, and it's a whole different scene—one that's kind of wild when you think about it.

Imagine you're at a table, maybe crushing some BBQ ribs or a loaded burger, and as soon as the fork's down, it's a straight shot to the car. You're gliding through traffic, headlights flicking past like ghosts, then boom—shoes off, body melted into the couch, hypnotized by a screen you're not even really watching. It's like a conveyor belt of sitting, no pause, no shift. Your body's stuck processing that feast with zero help, and your mind's just along for the ride, numbed out by the screen.

Anxiety is the enemy of a good meal. Whether you are planning a dinner party or sitting down for a quick bite alone, you cannot approach it anxiously. Instead, think of it as your chance to let go of fear and worry by focusing on the details of the present and the sensory experience of the food.

If you are looking forward to giving this approach a try, you can do it right now if you want. Put this book down. Clear your schedule for the next hour or two. Pick a place you enjoy eating. And go. Peruse the entire menu. Look at the ingredients under the different dishes. Pick something that sounds good but that you've never tried before. This is your call to adventure. Whether you end up liking it or not, you will have come out of the experience with something new. You will also have taken your first step into a larger world.

For those of you who can't wait to host a coursed-meal dinner party at your house, here's a simple step-by-step guide, based on the ideas above, that will help you take the guesswork (and anxiety) out of the prep.

1. **Set the scene:** Dim the lights. Throw on a playlist that says, "We've got taste but we're not trying too hard." Open a bottle of wine *before* the guests arrive so the mood is warm the second they walk in. No one wants to be greeted by the host yelling from the kitchen while wrestling with a corkscrew.

2. **Set the table:** Real plates. Glasses for both water and wine. Bread goes in a basket, not straight on the table as if you're camping. And yes, even on casual nights, there's usually a napkin (not a paper towel).

3. **Don't stress about the food:** Cook something you know well—comforting, seasonal, ideally something you can prep in advance. Nobody wants to watch you melt down over a risotto while they make awkward small talk with your cat. French hosts rarely serve something new or overly ambitious; they serve what they love and know how to execute without panic. Bonus points if it's a recipe passed down from someone's grandmother (which you're allowed to romanticize even if it's not true).

4. **Pace the evening:** The French love a proper *apéro*—drinks and little bites to kick things off. Think olives, radishes with butter and salt, chips (yes, chips), or a wedge of Comté cheese with some bread. You linger here. You chat. You refill glasses. No one rushes to the table. This warm-up phase might last thirty minutes... or an hour. Let it breathe.

5. **Serve things in courses, even if they're super simple:** A salad followed by a roasted chicken. A pot of something slow-cooked. Cheese. Dessert. The magic isn't in the menu—it's in the slowness. In France, dinner is the evening's entertainment. The table is the stage. So don't rush through it as if you've got somewhere better to be.

6. **Don't get up right after dessert:** You stay. You sip a digestif. Maybe espresso. You let the conversation wander. Hosting like a Frenchie means making your guests feel so comfortable they lose track of time—*and* so respected that they know exactly when the night is naturally winding down.

7. **Last thing: Don't clean up right away:** We know—it's tempting. But stacking plates midconversation kills the vibe. Let the mess live. It means the evening was good. Tidy up tomorrow. Tonight is for joy.

You don't need a Pinterest board to host like a Frenchie. You need warmth. A decent bottle of wine or sparkling water. Good lighting. Food you love. And a willingness to let go of control and just enjoy. Hosting isn't about perfection—it's about creating a space where people feel seen, heard, and well-fed.

Tom's Maman's Homemade Blanquette de Veau Maison

This is a total classic from the French kitchen, straight-up comfort food. Think tender chunks of veal, slow-simmered in a fragrant bath of dry white wine, jazzed up with a bouquet garni, juniper berries, and coriander seeds for that je ne sais quoi. The carrots, leeks, and whole onions (spiked with cloves, *très sophistiqué*—sophisticated) melt into the mix, while smoky lardons and earthy oyster mushrooms crash the party for some extra **chef's kiss**.

The sauce? A velvety dream—butter, cream, nutmeg, and a zesty lemon kick—all whisked to perfection, no lumps allowed, *s'il vous plaît* (please). Gluten-free? No stress, swap cornstarch for flour, and you're golden. Serve it with fluffy white rice or steamed potatoes to soak up that sauce, and you've got a dish that's pure French soul: rustic, refined, and ready to impress at any soirée. Bon appétit, *chérie*!

Ingredients (for 6 servings)

1.4 kg (3 lb) veal (shoulder, neck, breast, or flank; choose based on preference), cut into 5-cm (2-inch) pieces
150 g (5 oz) smoked bacon, cut into lardons
8 carrots, peeled and cut into large pieces
2 onions and 2 whole cloves
1 celery stalk, sliced

1 bouquet garni (thyme and bay leaf)
2 garlic cloves, crushed
75 cl (3 cups) dry white wine
1 tbsp salt
1 tbsp peppercorns
1 tbsp juniper berries
1 tbsp coriander seeds
2 tbsp tarragon white vinegar
4 leeks, sliced (to be added midway through)
200 g (7 oz) mushrooms (oyster mushrooms recommended by my mom)
60 g (4 tbsp) butter, divided
50 g (⅓ cup) flour or cornstarch (for gluten-free)
50 g (3½ tbsp) heavy cream (35% fat)
1 pinch nutmeg
Juice of 1½ lemons

Instructions

1. Prepare the vegetables: Wash, peel, and cut the carrots and celery into large chunks. Keep the onions whole, peel them, and stud each with a clove.

2. In a large pot, bring enough water to cover the veal (approximately 3 liters / 12 cups) to a boil, add the veal, and blanch for 5 minutes. After 5 minutes, remove the veal and drain until there is no more water.

3. In a Dutch oven, place the veal, onions, celery, bouquet garni, vinegar, garlic, and carrots.

Season with salt, peppercorns, juniper berries, and coriander seeds. Add the white wine and enough water to cover.

4. Bring to a simmer, then cook on low heat. After 1½ hours, add the leeks. Continue cooking on low for a total of 2 to 2½ hours.
5. Carefully remove the meat and vegetables, then strain the broth into a container and set aside.
6. In a cast-iron pot, melt 50 g (3½ tbsp) of butter gently. Off the heat, add the flour or cornstarch, stir, then cook gently for 2–3 minutes. Gradually add 1 liter of the reserved broth, then the cream, a splash of lemon juice, and a pinch of nutmeg. Whisk well to avoid lumps.
7. Taste the sauce and adjust seasoning with salt, pepper, or nutmeg as needed.
8. Return the meat and vegetables to the pot to reheat briefly.
9. In a skillet, melt 10 g (½ tbsp) of butter and sauté the fresh mushrooms and lardons for 5 minutes, seasoning with salt and pepper. Add them to the pot.
10. Let everything simmer on low for a few moments.
11. Serve with white rice or steamed potatoes.

Chapter 7.

KEEP STYLE SIMPLE

Avec Alex and Leanne Ansar

While French style is not uniform, there's still a sense that you should not leave the house in your pajamas. Even a run to the grocery store deserves a bit of respect, given that you're going to be out in public. This has to do with the contrasting sense of privacy we talked about—you don't bring the public into your private life, and you don't bring your private life (or home dress) into public.

That said, if you're picturing Paris as a 24-7 runway where everyone's strutting in haute couture—relax. Having style can look many different ways. You've got the more polished types in crisp linen and loafers. The practical ones, like Tom, in track pants and a faded tee can also hold their own (as long as they "look alive," so to speak). Most Parisians are drifting somewhere in between, mixing intention with ease.

Style, like love, isn't about following a script. It's about showing up as you are. It's about a few solid pieces—a well-cut blazer, jeans that hug you right, a scarf that's seen some years—worn often, with confidence. That's the trick, the whole magic of it. Confidence born of authenticity. Know how what you wear makes you feel, and dress to feel like yourself. Parisian or not, good style is all about owning your story.

So, you're standing in front of your closet, wondering how to bottle that cool Parisian vibe without moving to the Marais. How do you capture a look that's equal parts polished and nonchalant, like you just tossed on a blazer and somehow ended up looking like a fashion icon? That's where this chapter comes in—a guide to unlocking the secrets of French style, from the philosophy behind it to the wardrobe staples that make it sing.

But let's be real: We're not fashion gurus. Our expertise lies more in, say, ordering food than curating closets. That's why we've called in the big guns—our friend Leanne Ansar, a French-American model and style expert whose life and work make her the perfect guide to all things chic français. Please enjoy her expertise and incredible point of view.

MEET LEANNE ANSAR: STYLE EXPERT AND MODEL

I always felt like I lived between two worlds when it comes to style. Growing up, I split my time between the U.S. and France, and it shaped me in ways I didn't fully appreciate until I was older. In America, I'd wander through the mall, picking up $12 dresses that felt like a steal. They were bright, trendy, and fun—perfect for playing dress-up, for being whoever I wanted to be that day. But then summer would come, and I'd hop on a plane to France to stay with my cousin. That's when everything would shift.

I remember one summer meeting up with her in a little boutique. She was eyeing this dress—simple, with tiny stars scattered across it. It was 180 euros, and I nearly choked. Back home, that could've gotten me a whole wardrobe! But she just smiled, handed over her savings, and said it was worth it. That dress, she told me, was from a family business. You could trace every thread—where the fabric came from, who made it, how they were paid. It wasn't just a dress. It was a story, a commitment to quality. She wore it constantly, and it always looked effortless, elegant, like her. I started to get it: In France, it's not about having more—it's about having better. In an age of disposable fashion, I was raised, in part, on French values that clothes could be so personal they are indispensable.

That's when I began to see French style for what it is: a way of life. It's not loud or forced. It's natural, almost instinctive. It's having fewer options and a greater alignment between wardrobe and sense of self.

How do we get there? Let's discuss, beginning with the two biggest principles: achieving an effortless elegance and always feeling self-assured.

ELEGANCE THAT LOOKS EFFORTLESS

This is the foundation of French style. The goal is to look put together but never overdone. It's about achieving that "naturally stylish" appearance where it seems like you just threw something on without a second thought, even though you probably spent a lot of time carefully curating your outfit.

Riding the *métro* is like attending a daily master class in effortless style. When I rode, I studied commuters like some kids memorize football stats. A lawyer in a navy coat tailored to a razor's edge, every seam muffled precision. An art student in oversized vintage denim, paint-splattered and unbothered. A grandmother rocking pearls with a delicate blouse, her elegance so effortless it felt unreal. Nobody looked like they were trying too hard, yet every detail—cuff links, a rolled hem, the angle of a hat—was a deliberate choice, minimally executed, argued in silence.

This kind of elegance comes from refinement—in other

words, achieving maximum impact with a minimum of parts.

There's a famous quote, often attributed to Mark Twain in a letter to his lawyer: "Sorry I wrote such a long letter. I didn't have time to write a shorter one." This captures why looking effortless can be so hard—it requires stripping away the unnecessary. It's easier to write a ten-page letter that expresses all your thoughts than it is to condense it to five pages.

Finding elegance in your wardrobe is the same: You spend the necessary time to discard what is excessive and land on a carefully curated set of options, none of which is a wasted wear. It's about finding precision without excessive volume.

Take my basics—my holy grail. It took me some time to figure out what those pieces were for me, but now I know: Give me a perfect pair of classic blue jeans, a crisp white tee, and ballet flats, and I'm set. Maybe I'll throw on a black blazer if I'm feeling a little extra, or drape a sweatshirt over my shoulders for that perfect mix of polished and relaxed. It's not about reinventing the wheel every day. It's about knowing what works and owning it. I'd rather re-wear the same five pieces all week than chase a new look just for the sake of it.

French style taught me that elegance doesn't mean trying too hard. It's about transparency, quality, and a little bit of pride in knowing who you are. I'm not here to follow trends or change my look every season. I'm here to wear my story, one perfect piece at a time.

SELF-ASSURANCE: THE FINAL TOUCH

Avec Alex

French fashion isn't just about clothes—it's about the attitude you bring to them. When you own what you wear and carry yourself with ease, your outfit instantly looks more stylish.

One of my earliest memories is of my maman and me standing outside my primary school. She's smoothing the collar of my too-big winter coat, her breath visible in the chilly air as she whispers, "*Tiens-toi droit, mon chou, ça change tout.*" *Stand tall, sweetie, it changes everything.*

She wasn't wrong. Around here, the cut of a jacket or the knot of a scarf says a lot about you before you even open your mouth—your posture even more so. But it's not about wealth or labels—it's about signaling you know the game. If you slouch, you dishonor whatever clothes you may be wearing. Carry yourself well, and it does not matter what the labels say. You will scream confidence.

The playground hammered that lesson home for me, sharp and fast. I went to school with a lot of wealthy kids. They would march around in shiny, brand-new windbreakers like they ruled recess. Meanwhile, I was piecing together outfits from the *marché aux puces* (flea market) in Saint-Ouen, or digging through clearance bins for anything that didn't scream "hand-me-down." Money was tight, so I got scrappy. I'd swap out boring buttons for quirky ones I found at the flea market, roll up sleeves to fake a tailored fit, or hunt for vintage finds nobody could trace back to a bargain. At the end of the day, the kids with the fancy new fits held no further sway than I did, because I walked with self-respect and pride.

What started as a kid's survival tactic—don't look like the poor one—turned into fast maturity. I understood early what French adults understand en masse: Understated clothes and good posture convey more confidence than fancy new clothes alone ever will.

Tom is another great example of this. While I was rebelling with my flea-market hunts, his simplicity was its own kind of rebellion in an environment obsessed with aesthetics. Growing up, his wardrobe was 90 percent football gear—baggy football shirts he'd snag on summer trips to Morocco because Paris prices were a joke, tight track pants built for speed, and trainers tough enough for after-school pickup matches in the dust. If you tried talking to him about raw denim or shirt collars, he'd just shrug and say, "Mate, clothes are for moving, not posing."

For Tom, style was about function—gear that didn't slow him down or make him think twice. This was so true to who Tom was. You would never look at him and think he should be wearing anything else. And because of this confidence, he wore those outfits—they did not wear him.

Tom is proof you don't need a tailored trench to belong here—he's as Parisian as the guy in the Dior ad, just in his own way. I could not pull off Tom's style, because of how it would make me feel. To Tom, though, it's like a second skin, and he is more than proud to make that statement about himself with his shoulders back and his eyes sharp.

RULES FOR DRESSING LIKE A FRENCHIE

Okay, now that we understand the big goal of French fashion—to walk around feeling great about yourself while deploying a refined wardrobe curated to make you feel that way—let's look at how we can actually get there.

The Four Main Ingredients: Texture, Tone, Fabric, and Fit

Avec Leanne

Texture and fabric choices are a huge part of effortless style. The French favor natural, high-quality fabrics that age beautifully—soft cotton, luxurious cashmere, and supple leather, for example. A slightly worn-in jacket or a perfectly draped linen shirt can say more than a loud, trendy statement piece ever could. We're all about getting a good deal—but on great things. Paying less for cheap materials, crooked stitching, or shirts with misspelled words (the worst!) isn't a bargain. It's just a short-term fix.

Fabric weight is an important part of the equation as well. Just because a piece of clothing looks and feels good doesn't mean you'll enjoy wearing it if it makes you feel like you're suiting up for combat or on your way to the beach in the middle of a snowstorm. Consider the local climate, yes, but also consider your tendencies: Do you generally get overheated and end up stripping layers? Or are you someone who wears a light hoodie midday in summer? Know your own physiology and choose items you won't need to either strip away or add to based on how quickly your internal furnace fires or goes quiet.

Next up: color palettes. Black, white, navy, beige, and gray are the cornerstones of French fashion. These neutral shades create a refined and naturally coordinated look. A muted wardrobe allows for easy mixing and matching while maintaining an air of understated sophistication. We are all for subtle splashes of fun—throwing in a quirky bag, interesting belt buckle, colorful jewelry, or anything that will make you feel comfy and happy. We just don't go all out head to toe with it—flashy colors, bold neon tones, or clashing patterns are not our jam. There's no need for excessive branding, glittering embellishments, or over-the-top accessories either. Instead, it's the small, intentional details that make all the difference—a perfectly draped scarf, a well-chosen watch, or an artfully disheveled cuff.

Finally, think fit. In French fashion, the little details aren't just details—they are *everything*—and fit is one of the most important. Even the simplest outfit—a white shirt and jeans—can look incredibly chic when everything fits just right. The French understand that tailoring makes all the difference, which is why you'll rarely see an impeccably dressed Parisian drowning in oversized clothing or squeezed into something too tight. Proportion and structure matter, and knowing how to balance them is key.

So find a go-to tailor—essential when it comes to French style. Getting your T-shirts hemmed sounds crazy when you're buying in bulk, but when you're investing in only a few well-made tees, throwing in a couple extra dollars to make them just right isn't so insane. Trust us—try it, and you'll be hooked.

This leads directly into the next thing you want to keep in mind at all times.

Choose Quality Over Quantity

As you've probably gotten by now, the French don't believe in cramming their wardrobes with fast fashion pieces that lose their shape and charm after a few washes. Instead, they invest in well-made, timeless garments that stand the test of time. A beautifully tailored blazer or a classic pair of leather shoes will always be more valuable than a dozen trendy but cheaply made alternatives.

You are seeking a long-term relationship with your clothing, not a one-night stand. Don't just think twice before making a purchase. Think three, four, even five times! And don't be afraid of making returns. If you bring something home thinking it will make you feel a certain way about yourself, then you put it on to leave the house and the feeling isn't there, or worse, it makes you feel bad or hesitant in some way, trust your gut. Don't double down on a bad decision. Change back into one of those staples, put the receipt and the garment in your car, and drive that piece back from whence it came.

Quality doesn't mean brand new and/or designer either. If you get me started on vintage shopping in France, you may never get me to stop—it's practically an art form. There's nothing like digging through a thrift shop in Paris and finding a pair of perfectly worn-in jeans for thirty or forty euros. They've got history, character, and they're kinder to the planet. It's high luxury with a conscience, and it's always in style. French people get that. We love our vintage, our sustainability, because it's not just about looking good—it's about feeling good and knowing you're part of something bigger.

Don't Be Afraid to Mix Fashion

Avec Alex

When I was very young, around three years old, my parents divorced. My mom kept our apartment in the Seventeenth Arrondissement in Paris, and my dad moved to Versailles. So, much like Leanne, growing up I split my days between two places: Paris with my mom and Versailles with my dad. While they weren't as drastically different as the U.S. and France, they informed my sense of self-dress in the same way. I still reek of a blend of the gritty charm of the Batignolles district in Paris—where bistros spilled onto sidewalks and secondhand shops on the rue des Dames overflowed with faded treasures—and weekends in Versailles, where life slowed down to a crawl, the streets gleamed a little brighter, and strangers actually paused to say "Bonjour" with a nod.

Batignolles was all raw energy: the smell of fresh pastries, the hum of scooters, a vibration in the air reflecting the density of the population and utility of its buildings. It had its own flavor in terms of style: a barista in a thrifted leather jacket pouring coffee, a teenager in mismatched sneakers flirting by the crêpe stand, everyone speaking that silent language of fashion, saying something about who they are without a word.

Versailles felt like a deep breath by comparison, polished and serene, with manicured gardens, museum architecture, and old ladies in crisp scarves who'd smile like they knew your secrets. Those two worlds shaped me, each teaching me something about how to carry myself in a city that never stops watching. I'd watch the locals stroll through the market, their outfits simple but sharp, a hint of bourgeois: a wool coat over a plain sweater, boots polished but not flashy, a canvas tote slung over one shoulder.

The influence this had on me? I started mixing the two worlds: Versailles's quiet elegance, Batignolles's rough-around-the-edges charm. A secondhand blazer with a tee I'd had forever, or a flea-market scarf tied just so with trainers I'd worn through a hundred walks. It wasn't about perfection but about feeling like myself.

Mixing high and low fashion is another cornerstone of French style. A designer jacket paired with well-worn denim or a high-quality turtleneck matched with affordable boots creates a look that feels organic rather than ostentatious. For the French, it's not about flaunting wealth or status but about crafting an outfit that is balanced—proving that, again, true elegance isn't about price tags but about how you wear what you own.

Layer Carefully

Avec Leanne

Layering is a great way to put together an elegant, effortless look, but it should feel intentional—not like you're preparing for an extreme-weather survival challenge. You can layer with a mix of styles or just the basics—a well-fitted blazer over a sweater or a lightweight scarf paired with a classic coat, for example. The key is to find the perfect balance between warmth and elegance, and never overloading yourself to the point of resembling an overstuffed snowman.

You also want to avoid an obvious divorce in the making when marrying disparate pieces of wardrobe—like a classic trench and flip-flops. This is another reason it's important to keep your basics simple, so that they are adaptable. Like that one friend you never worry about fitting in with a new crowd.

Skip the Logos

Avec Alex

Want to know one of the biggest fashion faux pas? An overreliance on logos. French people don't parade around in oversized branding or loud designer emblems. They let the craftsmanship and fit of their clothing do the talking. The goal is for people to notice *you*, not just the label plastered across your chest. The idea of becoming a walking billboard for a brand is crazy in our culture. We have a lot to say, and we don't want our clothes to do the talking on our behalf.

Accessorize Intentionally

Avec Leanne

When putting the final touches on your outfit, don't overlook the little things. In the end, French fashion isn't about piling on expensive designer pieces—it's about attention to the details.

The way a sweater falls just right over a pair of classic jeans, the subtle gleam of a polished, clean sneaker, the spritz of a signature fragrance—all these little things add up to something greater than the sum of their parts. That's the secret of French style: It's about making every small choice count.

Accessories should always be chosen with care. A classic watch, a quality leather belt, and a few meaningful pieces of jewelry are all you need to elevate an outfit, and each accessory should serve a purpose rather than add unnecessary flair. Overaccessorizing is a common mistake that can make even the most well-curated ensemble look cluttered and contrived. A good practice might be taking one last glance in a mirror before heading out the door and asking yourself, "Does my eye go to one great accessory, or is my focus darting around, not knowing where to fall?" If it feels a little too much, it probably is.

Practice Good Grooming Habits

Avec Leanne

When it comes to men, grooming is the quiet architecture beneath great style—the part no one sees but everyone feels. Think of it as editing rather than embellishing, the goal being effortless sophistication. For example, messy, unwashed hair is a definite no, but so is an overly polished, slicked-back look. The sweet spot lies somewhere in between—slightly tousled yet well maintained.

The secret for men and women alike is a natural, low-maintenance routine that enhances rather than overwhelms. What does that routine consist of?

- Clear, hydrated skin (cleanser, moisturizer, SPF) makes every fabric look more expensive against it. Choose one active ingredient (vitamin C in the morning or a retinoid at night) and be consistent rather than experimental.
- Hair looks "effortless" because it's maintained: regular trims, a weekly mask, and small daily habits—boar-bristle brush to distribute oils, a touch of dry shampoo to lift the roots, a drop of serum on the ends. Sleep on a satin pillowcase, twist damp lengths into a loose bun for soft waves by morning, or slick a low pony with a dab of conditioner for shine.
- Brows are framed, not painted (tweeze strays; brush up with clear gel).
- Nails are trimmed and clean—buffed or a sheer polish is plenty.
- Finally, you smell good: Fresh breath, deodorant, and a whisper of fragrance on pulse points—not a cloud—finish the impression of being put together without trying too hard.

Technique-wise, keep a five-minute reset you can do on autopilot: splash of water, lip balm, brow gel, hand cream or cuticle oil, lint roller, quick steam of whatever you're wearing.

French Men Do Fashion

Take a walk through Paris, and you'll see it: men looking as if they've been styled for a fashion magazine. They'll spend a little extra time on their self-care: hair neatly done, maybe a subtle spritz of cologne, and nails that are actually manicured. To some cultures, this might read as "feminine" or raise an eyebrow, with assumptions about sexuality or vanity. But French men? They shrug it off. They're not fazed by the side-eye. Why? Because they're not dressing to dodge judgment; they're dressing to express themselves. That extra thought they put into looking chic isn't about insecurity. It's about pride in their craft, like an artist perfecting a canvas.

When it comes to style, the French have a kind of fearless authenticity that sets them apart, and nowhere is this more evident than in how French men approach fashion. They don't dress to please others or to fit into some rigid mold of what a man "should" look like; they dress for themselves, with a confidence that's as liberating as it is magnetic. French men have a swagger that says, "I know I look good, and I don't care what you think."

This attitude ties back to a deeper French philosophy: honesty over approval. French men aren't out here chasing trends or worrying about seeming "tough" enough to satisfy some outdated playbook. They'll wear a pink shirt or a slim-cut suit because it feels right, not because it checks a box. It's not arrogance; it's clarity. They know who they are, and their style is an extension of that, not a performance for someone else's validation.

Other cultures might misread this confidence, but that's their loss. Other guys might scoff at a man carrying a leather satchel or wearing a velvet blazer, as if it's somehow "less masculine." In France, those same choices are just . . . normal.

Again, it's not about proving anything—it's about living with intention. They're not afraid to stand out, even if it means standing alone. And honestly, that's what makes their chic so powerful: It's rooted in a quiet certainty that doesn't need anyone else's nod of approval. They're authentic, unapologetically themselves, and in a world obsessed with fitting in, that's the boldest statement of all.

BUILDING YOUR FRENCH WARDROBE

Avec Leanne

Inspired by the streets of Paris, where every outfit tells a story, here's a guide to building a wardrobe that channels that French chic, no matter where you are. Each of these items is a building block, versatile and timeless, with a nod to the confidence that makes French fashion iconic.

The Perfect White Shirt: Your Wardrobe's Best Friend

A crisp white button-down is the ultimate French essential, working for everyone—men, women, anyone who loves a clean silhouette. Tucked into tailored trousers for a meeting, untucked with jeans for a café date, or sleeves rolled up for a casual stroll, it's endlessly adaptable. The key? Fit and fabric. It should skim your body, not cling or sag, and stay crisp enough to say "I've got this" without shouting. Just iron it—wrinkles scream "lost tourist" louder than a fanny pack. Pair it with confidence, and it's your secret weapon for any occasion.

Tailored Blazer: Instant Elegance, No Effort Required

A blazer is your wardrobe's magic wand, turning a basic outfit into something that says, "I just threw this on, but I look *impeccable*." Think *parfaitement* (perfectly) chic. Whether it's navy for classic vibes, black for edge, or a soft gray for versatility, the fit is everything—tailored to your shoulders, nipping in at the waist. Toss it over a tee and jeans for drinks or pair it with a skirt for work—it's the difference between ordinary and extraordinary. Choose quality over flash, and let it do the talking.

Breton Striped Shirt: The Classic Marinière

The Breton striped shirt—navy and white, born of French sailors—is a Parisian staple, but it's not a costume. It's about wearing it with quiet confidence, not shouting, "I'm French!" Pair it with dark denim and a leather jacket for a night out, or tuck it into chinos for a weekend brunch. The trick is balance: Keep the rest of the outfit simple to let the stripes shine.

Well-Fitted Jeans: The Foundation of Cool

French jeans are about fit, not flash—slim but not skinny, straight-leg, or slightly cropped for a touch of flair. They hug you just right, moving with you whether you're biking along the Seine or sipping wine at a bistro. Avoid overly distressed styles unless you're actually headlining a rock show. I pair my dark-wash, high-waisted jeans with a tucked-in blouse and boots, looking polished yet relaxed. Invest in a pair that feels like a second skin, and they'll carry you through any day with effortless cool.

Black Turtleneck: Intellectual Meets Mysterious

The black turtleneck is French style's secret weapon, making you look like you're pondering Sartre or have just nailed a poetry reading—even if you're just debating olive oil versus butter. It's sleek, timeless, and works for everyone. Pair it with tailored trousers for a gallery vibe or jeans for a casual edge. The key is quality—choose a soft, fitted fabric that feels luxurious. It's not just clothing; it's a mood.

Classic Trench Coat: Your Armor Against the Ordinary

A trench coat is the ultimate French outerwear, screaming, "I have my life together!" even if you just spilled coffee on your shirt. Beige, navy, or olive, it's versatile enough for rain-soaked mornings or crisp evenings. Belt it for structure or leave it open for nonchalance. Choose one with clean lines and a length that hits mid-thigh for maximum impact. It's not just a coat—it's a statement of quiet confidence.

Ballet Flats or Loafers: Timeless Footwear for All

Ballet flats for women and sleek loafers for men (or anyone) are French style staples, blending comfort with class. They say, "I appreciate good wine and even better conversation." Women can pair flats with jeans or a dress; men can rock loafers with chinos or a suit. Swap sneakers for loafers, and they'll up your game—trust us.

Chic Boots: Worn In, Never Overdone

Chelsea boots, leather ankle boots, or suede desert boots—French style demands footwear that's stylish but lived-in, not shiny and new. They should look like they've seen a few Paris streets but still hold their own at a dinner party. Pair them with jeans or a dress for women, or chinos and a blazer for men. Choose quality leather and a versatile color like black or brown to wear them year-round with everything.

Silk Scarf: A Touch of Artful Sophistication

A silk scarf is the French accessory that whispers, "*I know art, I read books, and I might own a vintage bicycle*"—even if you don't. Tie it around your neck, drape it over a blazer, or knot it onto a bag for instant polish. Every chic Parisian woman has a collection she's built over decades, each scarf adding a pop of personality to her simple outfits. Go for subtle patterns or bold colors, but keep it silk for that luxurious feel. It's the easiest way to look like you've mastered the art of chic.

Minimalist Handbag or Messenger Bag: Carry Class, Not Clutter

A high-quality leather bag—tote for women, messenger or satchel for men—is a French must-have. It's about carrying the essentials with elegance, not lugging around an overstuffed backpack. Choose a sleek design in black, tan, or navy that pairs with everything. Invest in something durable, and let it age beautifully—it's not just a bag; it's a companion for life's adventures.

A Signature Scent: Always Leave an Impression

The French understand that true elegance isn't only about what you wear—it's about how you make people feel, and scent is a powerful way to leave an impression.

Fragrance is the invisible yet unforgettable finishing touch in French fashion and style. It's not just an accessory but is part of who you are. It becomes a signature, a personal statement that lingers long after you've left the room.

As you've learned well by now, French style is all about effortlessness, and the same rule applies to fragrance. The best scents are worn with restraint—just a dab on the pulse points, maybe a hint on the collar. It's never about announcing yourself from across the room but about creating an intimate, sensory experience for those who come close. You'd be surprised how often people remember you for how you smell.

Scent also plays a psychological role in fashion and self-presentation—the right fragrance can make you feel and come across as more confident, put-together, and even seductive. A crisp citrus or woody scent can radiate sophistication, while deeper notes of leather or spice can add mystery and depth. The right scent doesn't just complement your style—it *becomes* part of your story.

Berets and Other French Fashion Stereotypes

If the image of French style still conjures up a red-lipped lady wearing a beret while walking a French poodle with one hand and holding a cigarette in the other, crossing under the Eiffel Tower . . . you're missing the mark. Cliché French styles (think berets, blue-and-white striped sweaters, red scarves, and trench coats) are like snapshots from a vintage postcard—they're iconic, romanticized, and often tied to a certain vision of France peddled by pop culture. But do French people actually wear them?

The Beret: The ultimate French stereotype—slanted ever so on the head, evoking artists, poets, or maybe a mime. Historically, berets were practical headwear for Basque farmers, adopted by the French military and later the cultural elite in the early twentieth century. Today? They're not a daily staple. You might spot a beret in artsy Parisian neighborhoods like Montmartre or on someone deliberately channeling a retro vibe, but most Frenchies aren't tossing one on for their morning coffee run. It's more tourist gift shop than local wardrobe—worn ironically or for a themed photo shoot rather than as a go-to. Still, during fashion weeks or in vintage-inspired outfits, a beret can pop up, styled with a modern edge.

Blue-and-White Striped Sweater (*Marinière*): This one's got legit roots. Originally the uniform of Breton sailors in the nineteenth century, the *marinière* was popularized by Coco Chanel in the 1910s. Its clean lines scream "French cool." Do

French people wear it? Yes, but not as a uniform. It's a classic piece, especially in coastal areas like Brittany or among those who love nautical-inspired looks. In cities, you'll see it layered under blazers or paired with jeans, but it's not everywhere. The French lean toward muted, versatile pieces, so the *marinière* fits right in—just don't expect every Parisian to be rocking one.

Red Scarf: The bright red scarf tied around the neck is a cinematic trope—think Amélie or a heroine strolling the Seine. Scarves are huge in France, but red ones aren't the default. French women and men love scarves in all colors—silk for polish, wool for warmth—knotted with careless precision. A red scarf might appear, especially in autumn or for a pop of color, but it's not a cliché they lean into daily. It's more about personal flair than a national dress code.

Trench Coat: Beige, belted, and billowing as someone dashes through a rainy Paris street—this one's a cliché with staying power. Born from military origins (Burberry and Aquascutum made them for World War I soldiers), the trench became a French style hallmark thanks to its practicality and elegance. Do the French wear it? Absolutely. It's a wardrobe staple, especially in spring and fall when the weather's moody. Walk around any French city, and you'll see trenches everywhere—on women cinching them over dresses, on men pairing them with sneakers. It's less about cliché and more about function meeting timeless style.

Other Clichés: Black turtlenecks (hello, existentialist vibes) are tied to 1960s intellectuals and artists like Juliette Gréco. They're still worn, especially by creative types or anyone building a minimalist look. Ballet flats? Chanel made them iconic, and yes, they're a French favorite—comfy, chic, and perfect for walking (which, as we've noted, the French love). The baguette-toting, bike-riding Parisian in a striped dress? More Hollywood than reality, though you'll see chic dresses and bikes—just not always with a loaf of bread as a prop.

Here's the deal: French style isn't about clichés; it's about authenticity. Some of these stereotypical items, like trenches and flats, are genuinely popular because they're practical and versatile, aligning with that "quality over quantity" mindset we love to embody. Others, like berets or overly matchy striped looks, are more niche—embraced by a few, exaggerated by media. The French don't wake up thinking, "How can I look super French today?!" They just live, and their style follows—nonchalant, intentional, and unbothered by stereotypes.

By now we hope you've grasped that styling yourself like the French isn't simply about looking chic—it's about feeling well. Clothes, when chosen with thought, become more than fabric. They become a form of self-respect. Dressing with intention fuels confidence. A blazer shrugged over denim or a scarf tied with quiet precision sends a message: *I value myself.* That small act of care echoes throughout your day, lifting your mood, shaping your posture, even altering how you interact with others.

French fashion is also a practice in simplicity—quality

over quantity, curation over clutter. A wardrobe made up of pieces you truly love clears both your closet and your mind. It's one fewer decision to drain your energy in the morning, freeing space for everything else that matters.

And let's not forget comfort. French style insists that elegance doesn't come at the cost of ease. Shoes you can walk in, fabrics that breathe, cuts that allow movement—these are not indulgences but essentials. When you're physically comfortable, your body isn't fighting against what you're wearing, which leaves you more energized, more focused, more at ease in your skin.

Perhaps most important, the French treat getting dressed as a ritual of self-care. Grooming, accessorizing, and even slipping into a crisp white shirt is as much about honoring yourself as it is about how the world sees you. The effect is twofold: You feel aligned internally, and you present to the world a version of yourself that invites respect and connection.

In the end, style is not a shallow pursuit. It is a quiet but powerful pillar of wellness—a daily practice of confidence, simplicity, comfort, and self-respect. And no one embodies this balance better than the French.

Chapter 8.

BUILD FRIENDSHIPS THAT LAST

Avec Tom

"You'll see when you grow up," my dad told me one day. "In the end, you'll only have five people you can truly call *tes amis* (your friends)."

When I was about twelve years old, that sounded restrictive. Just five? I had way more friends than that, and I was only twelve! It felt like some old-man rule—but my dad stuck to it. His reasoning was that fewer than five meant you were too isolated, and more than five meant you didn't have time to build anything real. Small circles are where the good stuff grows—loyalty, depth, the things you can count on when the world goes sideways.

As I got older, I started to see what my dad meant. Friendships naturally faded, not because of drama or fallouts but because with time I learned to choose depth over numbers. I realized not everyone deserves my all. Nor am I capable of giving everything to everyone. It's simply not possible when you are restricted by time, distance, shared interests, or moral character. People are too diverse a species for us all to be best friends with each other. So I stopped trying to keep up with everyone and focused on the ones who truly cared about me just as much as I cared about them.

It turns out, my dad was right.

FRIENDSHIP THE FRENCH WAY

In French culture, friendship isn't about racking up acquaintances; it's about building something real. You don't instantly become someone's best friend. You show up again and again—to dinners, on rainy walks, over long conversations. It's less "How fast can we bond?" and more "How well do we hold each other over time?"

It's also not about how many people you know but how well you know them. We carefully curate our inner circle, much like a Michelin-starred chef selecting the finest ingredients. We'd rather have a few *les amis* (those ride-or-die types you trust with your ugliest secrets) than a hundred *les copains* (the people you can enjoy a drink and share a laugh with but not turn to in a crisis). That tight circle mirrors my dad's logic: Keep it small, keep it real.

Privacy is huge for my dad, as by now you know it is for the French. It applies to friendships: You don't unwrap your wounds in the open or offer your depth to those just skimming the surface. Trust grows in close quarters, away from the spotlight—just as Dad wanted me to guard my circle from the chaos of a bigger crowd.

Montaigne once wrote about his friendship with La Boétie, "Parce que c'était lui, parce que c'était moi." *Because it was him, because it was me.* That's the level of depth and simplicity the French value. Not performative, just true.

Which means relationships aren't just something you maintain when it's convenient—they're the foundation of everything. You don't just have friends. You invest in them. You show up. You call. You meet. You help. You stay longer than you planned. You love. The French don't treat connection as a luxury or an extra. It's a necessity, like breathing, like eating.

The truth is, I didn't realize how lucky I was to have the friends I did. I think we often believe that friendship is mostly about the laughter, the memories, the inside jokes. But real friendship, *les amis*, is also much quieter than that. It's about who stays when the excitement fades. Who remembers how to care for you when you've forgotten how to care for yourself. Who you haven't seen in a while but still feels like yesterday when you reconnect. That kind of friendship doesn't look dramatic. It looks stable. *Mes amis* keep me sane. They keep me motivated. They remind me who I am.

Alex and I have been through many similar experiences in our lives—some of them happy, others not—but we have always had each other to talk, share, listen, laugh, debate, grow, sit in silence, and breathe with, and, most important, to understand each other. Everything that we have done and experienced since the first day we met has led to the relationship we share. It wasn't built in a rush or with grand gestures. It grew slowly, over time, through trust, honesty, and showing up for one another. That's the kind of bond that doesn't need to be explained. It just is. It's the quiet certainty that no matter what happens next, we will continue to lift each other up and bring out the best in ourselves.

Don't get me wrong—building this kind of closeness isn't always easy. Schedules clash. Distance happens. Sometimes it's months between seeing each other. But the depth doesn't fade. *Les amis* allow for the pauses, they respect your growth, your space, your silence—and still hold you close. That's why these five, these *amis*, are so rare.

If I ever have kids, I will make sure to tell them the same thing: "You'll have only five real friends." Not as a warning but as a hope that they'll know the richness of depth real friends can bring. As a hope that they'll find their people, their chosen family, and build something real. As a hope that I will be more than a dad to them, I'd like to be their friend, as well.

ALONE, YOU'RE LOST; IN A PACK, YOU'RE HOME: A QUICK HISTORY LESSON

Our obsession with connection isn't new to French culture—it's carved into our history, deep as the grooves in a medieval cobblestone street. Rewind to feudal France: villages scattered across the countryside, stone cottages huddled around a communal oven. That oven wasn't just for bread—it was the heart of the hamlet, where villagers swapped gossip about who nabbed Pierre's goat or who spiked the cider too hard. Survival wasn't a solo sport. It was a team effort. You leaned on your kin—cousins, grandparents, that one uncle whom nobody liked—or you didn't make it through winter.

Fast-forward to the French Revolution, and that spirit got a glow-up. *Liberté, égalité, fraternité*—liberty, equality, brotherhood—wasn't just a slogan to slap on a flag. Brotherhood was the real deal. Liberty's hot, equality's noble, but community? That's the heartbeat that made the other two tick.

The Declaration of the Rights of Man and of the Citizen, adopted in August 1789 during the early stages of the French Revolution, sent shock waves beyond France and throughout the world, fundamentally reshaping the idea of human rights on a global scale. While it wasn't the first document to talk about rights, its timing, scope, and universal framing made it a tipping point. The declaration didn't just redefine legal and political rights—it reshaped social bonds by introducing new ideas to the French, such as declaring human rights as natural, inalienable, and universal—not something granted disproportionately by rulers. Sure, they were cribbing the preamble to the U.S.'s own Declaration of Independence, but this idea coming from France had a broader influence. It really springboarded the adoption of Western principles of individualism, liberty, equality, and fraternity throughout Europe.

In France, this shift in perspective fundamentally altered the way individuals saw themselves, their rights, their values, and subsequently, their roles in society. Ironically, this shift toward individualist thinking brought people closer together as a whole. We learned everyone has the same value regardless of social standing. We learned it through blood and barricades: Alone, you're toast; together, you've got a shot.

Post–World War II, same story—rebuilding from rubble meant leaning on neighbors, sharing what little you had, from a sack of potatoes to a quiet nod that said, "We'll get through this." It's why we'll still shut down Paris over pension reforms, strike collectively, or argue till dawn over politics at a dive bar. We're not lone wolves. We're individual members of a loud and unbreakable pack, formed around the idea that we all have value and that our individual rights are something we are born with, not something bestowed upon us that can be taken away.

Even our cities tell the tale. Paris spirals outward in circles, the oldest bits at the core, like a history lesson in brick and stone. Walk from the outer arrondissements to the center, and you're stepping backward through time—a metaphor for how we huddle inward, drawing strength from roots while stretching into the now. Compare that to cultures where it's all "pull yourself up by your bootstraps"—no shade, but we'd rather split a pot of stew with our *copains* than starve proving we don't need anyone.

To us, codependence isn't a weakness. It's a strength, a safety net woven through centuries of surviving together. It's why we value the collective over the solitary—because we know nobody makes it alone, not really.

That historical pack mentality plays out in how we live today, in rituals and rhythms that put people over productivity. Start with *l'apéro*, the sacred predinner hour where you crack open a pastis or rosé, toss some charcuterie on the table, and let the day's chaos melt into chatter. In the States, they call this happy hour, but it's often more about cheap drinks and quick chats. Nothing like the laid-back, relaxed social vibe of *l'apéro*.

Then there's our café culture, the original social network. We don't do grab-and-go. We linger. Nobody can stretch an espresso into a forty-five-minute chat session quite like the French.

Local markets are another opportunity to connect. In France, we're not drawn to vast, impersonal shopping malls. Instead, we rely on our trusted specialists: a butcher for the finest cuts, a baker for the perfect baguette, and local *marchés* for everything else. Our shops are small, intimate, often family owned, and deeply personal. You may not be friends with the shopkeepers, but growing up around them fosters a sense of community where everyone feels seen. Daily errands become opportunities for social connection, whether it's chatting with your local hairdresser or staying loyal to a favorite pastry chef. Supporting these small businesses matters to us. French people will happily pay a premium to keep their money with a family operation rather than a faceless corporation.

Family traditions hit even harder. Every Bastille Day, families pack into homes. You know the scene—too many cousins, not enough chairs. We fight over who lights the bonfire, then keep it going until midnight. It's chaos, but it's ours. Even modern rituals, like underground hip-hop nights in Belleville or pickup football (soccer) in the *banlieues* (suburbs), keep the thread tight. City or country, it's all about showing up together.

FRIENDSHIP IS BUILT THROUGH GESTURES, NOT PROMISES

At the heart of French social culture lies a simple principle we keep coming back to over and over: quality over quantity. As I mentioned, we tend to distinguish between two types of friends—*amis* and *copains*. *Amis* are the ride-or-die crew, the ones you call when life splits open at the seams. *Copains* are for lighter moments, good for a pint and a playlist, but not for the deep cuts. Mixing them up leads to trouble—expect a *copain* to show up when your world's imploding, and you might find yourself ghosted. So, we keep our circles tight and our expectations clear.

Most people start as *copains*. It takes time, trust, and a growing connection to turn them into *amis*. Trust isn't given lightly; it's built through actions, not words. We're guarded at first—not unfriendly, just selective. Don't expect us to stroll the streets flashing smiles at strangers. If we smile at you, it means we're comfortable, that you're in. Maybe that's where the "rude French" stereotype comes from—a cultural miscommunication, nothing more.

We also don't toss the word *friend* around casually. We've already got our pack, built over years of shared moments together. There's no desperate need to let new people in. But if it happens, and the fit feels right, then wonderful.

It isn't perfect, though; we'll admit that. Tight circles can feel cliquey, and newbies sometimes struggle to crack the code, especially in situations where everyone's known each other since diapers. And there's pressure to show up, even when you're tapped out. Skip too many *apéros*, and that uncle you despise will start asking if you're "too good" for the fam. But the trade-off? A life where you're rarely solo in the fight, where the collective buzz—be it a protest or a party—grounds you in something bigger. Social bonds outweigh ambition every time. A good hang isn't something we squeeze in. It's the main event.

And we give as much as we get. In Paris, I've seen neighbors drop off soup when someone's sick, or drag a friend to a gallery opening because they know they're in a funk. It's not duty—it's instinct, building trust one gesture at a time.

L'histoire d'Alex

Friendships Are Slow-Brewing

Growing up, I had this friend named Mathis, my partner in crime from age ten to about fifteen or sixteen. We were inseparable, kicking around the neighborhood, dreaming big and laughing at nothing. But then life threw a curveball—I got accepted into the Dijon soccer academy.

I'll admit it, I was a bit of a *crâneur* back then, a cocky teenager with stars in my eyes. I started chasing a new crowd, all soccer obsessed, thinking I was too cool for my old crew. Poor Mathis, I just . . . ghosted him. No big goodbye, no explanation, just a dumb kid being, well, dumb. We had a fight before I left—nothing major, just the kind of raw, direct clash you get when you're young and fiery, laying it all bare. And then I was gone.

Fast-forward ten years, and I'm in a bar in Paris when suddenly, I spot him. Mathis! He's not the scrawny kid I remember. He's shot up to like six foot three, towering over me. Yet the second our eyes meet, it's like we're fifteen again, back on our Vélib' bikes, causing mischief. Here's the magic of French friendship: Even after a decade of radio silence, the cork pops and the conversation flows effortlessly. He knows my whole story: my parents, my struggles, every awkward phase I went through. And I know his. We're laughing, reminiscing, spilling our guts about the last decade. It's not surface-level chitchat. It's deep, the kind of bond that doesn't rust.

That night, Mathis had nowhere to crash—his sister and mom were visiting that weekend and staying at his little studio. Without thinking, I was like, "Don't get a hotel; stay at mine." So there we were, sprawled in my apartment, drinking wine from 3 a.m. to 7 a.m., talking about how stupid we were back then. I apologized for ditching him, and he just shrugged. Then he drops a bombshell: His phone password is still my birthday—0724. After all these years! I made him unlock it to prove it, and my mind was blown. Here we were, two guys who hadn't spoken in a decade, picking up right where we left off, no grudges, no fakeness.

Since that night, we've been tight like it's 2016 again. We text, we grab beers, we're back in each other's lives. And that's when it hit me: This is the French friendship stereotype flipped on its head. From the outside, we look reserved—maybe even distant. But we're just aging the wine. We don't rush to call someone *ami* because, for us, that word means, "I'll help you move apartments in the rain," "I'll show up at the hospital at 2 a.m.," or "I'll bail you out of whatever mess." It's a lifetime warranty, not a casual label.

I've met plenty of casual friends over the years, the kind you bump into and share a laugh with. In French, we'd call them *potes*—fun, easygoing—but if they needed a place to crash at 3 a.m., I might hesitate. And that's okay—they're not bad people, they're just not *amis*. Mathis is my legit friend. He's the guy who'd have my back, and I'd have his, no questions asked. Having him back in my life reminds me that real French friends are like a home you can return to, no matter how far you've wandered or how many years you've been gone.

So next time someone tells you it's impossible to make friends in France, remember: We're not gate-keeping; we're slow-brewing. Give it time, share some stories, survive an adventure or two together, and one day you'll wake up to find you've crossed that precious line. And once you're an *ami*, you're uncorked for life.

Santé (cheers) to friendships that age well—and to the patience that makes them unforgettable.

HOW TO BUILD YOUR CIRCLE OF *AMIS*

This kind of friendship isn't some out-of-reach ideal you can't touch. It's real, lived-in, and you can find it for yourself. Here's our playbook for building a strong circle of *amis*.

Widen the Net

Join something local—a sports team, a book club—and while there, ask people questions to get the conversation going. Sign up for a class—kickboxing, pottery, whatever gets you out of the cave. The first step to making friends is showing up.

Start Small

For those who feel they're "not that social"—we hear you, and we're not here to drag you kicking and screaming into a spotlight. Not everyone's wired to be the loudmouth cracking jokes and clinking glasses with strangers, and that's cool. You don't need to charm a whole bar. Our advice? Start with one person you're already comfy with: a sibling, an old friend, or even a coworker who doesn't make you want to claw your eyes out. Ask them for a casual hang, nothing big—a beer after work, a lap around the park, an errand run, or just a coffee around your kitchen table. No script, no pressure, just twenty or thirty minutes of chitchat. Still feels like a stretch? Cut it to fifteen. It's not about draining your battery; it's about dipping into connection and feeling that slow warmth creep in.

Create Micro-Links

The server who knows your order, the barista at your go-to coffee shop, the old dude at the park with stories—these are all micro-links that can help you feel rooted in your community. While they might not necessarily become your forever best friend (and in fact, you may never see them again), that's not the point. It's about sharing a pleasant interaction that makes you feel seen, known, and connected.

Unplug to Plug In

Your phone's a leash—cut it loose. Next time you're eating with someone, make it a no-screen zone. Stack all the phones in the middle if you have to. Constant pings yank you out of the moment. In fact, certain studies tie heavy phone use to anxiety spikes and trash sleep.

At our hangouts, it's law: no screens, just faces. Try it for one meal—taste your food, catch the whole story, make eye contact. We are constantly "on" when we are digitally plugged in. Start small: one phone-free hour a day, maybe over dinner or a morning stroll. You'll catch what you've been missing—like your friend's laugh breaking midstory, or how your head quiets down when it's not always on alert.

Shop Small

Shop at small, family-owned businesses for things like baked goods, spices, and eggs over impersonal superstores. It's not just about buying goods; it's about fostering relationships with your community, supporting neighbors, and preserving a village mentality, even in big, international cities. Start by seeking out local farmers' markets, independent grocers, or small retailers in your area. Prioritize quality and personal ties over convenience, even if it means spending a bit more or taking extra time. Over time, these choices can cultivate a tighter-knit community, where every purchase strengthens the social fabric and makes the everyday feel more human.

Give to Get

Connection's a two-way street—we don't just take; we build. Pick up the phone after your girlfriend's rough day and shoot her a dumb meme to crack her up. It's not always big moves—sometimes it's just showing up, again and again, when a friend is in need to celebrate or commiserate. When you stumble—job loss, heartbreak, gray-ass winter days—there'll be a hand to yank you up if you've been that hand, too.

Find the Time

"Too busy" is the big one, right? We're swamped, barely keeping our heads above water, with no time for a proper chat. If you can carve out an hour to scroll TikTok, get lost in group texts, or binge the same sitcom episode for the third time, you've got room to shift gears. The French squeeze two-hour lunch breaks into a workday without blinking, so you can absolutely snag thirty minutes to visit a friend instead of just liking their post and pretending that counts. It's not about magically finding time but about redirecting the hours you're already frittering away on stuff that leaves you empty. We advise you to pick one night a week to swap screen time for a real convo. Invite a friend over for a chat on the couch—nothing fancy needed. Or a FaceTime while folding laundry or walking the dog works, too.

Connection's not a luxury here; it's soul fuel. Next time you catch yourself in a social media spiral, trade or balance it for a quick catch-up call with a friend. You'll feel it—less frazzled, more alive—without adding a single minute to your day.

Ritualize Moments That Matter

Turn basic hangouts into something sacred. Round up your crew not for delivery or takeout but to cook something together. Don't stress perfection—a pot of pasta with canned sauce does the trick. It's the act—chopping, stirring, creating together—that counts. Crank some tunes, crack a cheap bottle, and let the night breathe. Skip the small talk and dive into what's real: what's got you hyped, what's got you down. Face-to-face beats texting every time. In fact, science says in-person encounters release more oxytocin, the bonding juice, than digital ones. So set a date, pick a dish, make it a thing—your soul will feel fuller than an escargot.

Tighten Your Crew

You don't need a million followers—just a squad who feels like home. Acknowledge your *amis*. Three's a solid number, but if one is all you've got, that works, too! They don't need to be perfect, but they better show up when you're down and stick it out through the mess. Become each other's lifeline: weekly check-ins, random meetups, the kind of bond where you don't need a script. Studies show even a few close ties can slice through loneliness and make you bulletproof for life's curveballs.

Deepen Conversations with Friends

Looking for a way to turn a *copain* into an *ami*? Deepen your conversations. The French believe conversations should flow naturally, revealing who you are through stories and ideas. The following questions—focusing on fostering authentic, present connections—can help you uncover what makes your friends tick and foster the kind of intimacy that makes relationships lasting and real.

You may read this and think, *Wow, I've never even asked my amis these questions.* But give it a try. It might feel a little weird at first, but trust us, it's worth it.

- *What's a memory from your childhood that shaped who you are today?*
    - Why it works: This invites friends to share a formative story, opening the door to personal insights without being too direct.
- *If you could wake up tomorrow and be an expert in one thing, what would it be and why?*

  - Why it works: This taps into passions and dreams. It's playful yet revealing, showing what your friend values—creativity, adventure, knowledge—without feeling like an interrogation.

- *What's something you've always wanted to try but haven't, and what's holding you back?*
  - Why it works: This question emphasizes authenticity, encouraging friends to admit fears or hesitations.

- *When was the last time you felt truly alive, and what were you doing?*
  - Why it works: Inspired by the French focus on living in the moment, this question uncovers what brings your friend joy or adrenaline.

- *What's a belief you've changed your mind about over time, and what made you rethink it?*
  - Why it works: This digs into personal growth and invites reflection on how experiences shape perspectives, encouraging a friend to share a transformative moment without judgment.

- *If you could spend a day with anyone, living or not, who would it be, and what would you talk about?*
  - Why it works: This question taps into imagination and values, similar to the French love for meaningful conversation over coffee. It reveals who inspires your friend and what matters to them—history, art, family—while keeping the vibe light and open-ended.

- *What's something you're proud of that you don't often talk about?*
  - Why it works: The French value understated pride. This question gives your friend permission to share a quiet achievement—a project, a kind act—without feeling boastful, deepening your understanding of their character.
- *What's a place that feels like home to you, and what makes it so special?*
  - Why it works: This question uncovers emotional anchors, inviting friends to share what grounds them, whether it's a physical place or a feeling.
- *What's a challenge you're facing right now, and how are you navigating it?*
  - Why it works: This question aligns with the French directness, where honesty is delivered with finesse. It shows you care about their struggles without prying, creating a safe space for them to open up.
- *What's a dream you've never told anyone, and what would it take to chase it?*
  - Why it works: The chapter emphasizes "l'amour subtil"—subtle, meaningful gestures that show you see someone. Asking about a secret dream invites vulnerability, encouraging your friend to share a hidden hope, much like the quiet moments that define French romance.

At its heart, French friendship reminds us that depth beats breadth every time. Real connection is measured not by how many names are in your contacts list but by how many people show up when it matters most. The lesson is simple yet radical in a world obsessed with growing your network at speed: Guard your circle, invest in it, and let it grow slowly. Just as a strong adhesive takes time to set, so do the strong bonds that carry us through life's highs and lows.

True *amis* aren't just companions for laughter or nostalgia—they're the anchors in our storms, the ones who understand the unspoken, who respect our silence as much as our words. Building these relationships requires presence, patience, and reciprocity. It means putting down the phone, making time, showing up even when it's inconvenient, and giving as much as you hope to receive. In France, these gestures are not extras. They are the very foundation of belonging.

If you walk away with one principle from this chapter, let it be this: A handful of real *amis* will enrich your life more than a hundred casual connections ever could. In a pack, you find your home—stable, steady, and unshakably yours.

Part III

THE FRENCH ART OF APPRECIATING LIFE

COMMENT VOIR LA BEAUTÉ DANS LE QUOTIDIEN

How to see the beauty hidden in everyday life

There's a moment, usually somewhere around the second coffee of the morning or during the golden-hour walk home, when life slows down just enough for you to actually *notice* it. The color of the sky. The shape of a shadow. The way a stranger's laugh lifts the air. That's the start of living the French way, too—not in grand gestures but in tiny, deliberate acts of attention.

If part 1 taught you how to *think* like the French, and part 2 showed you how to *love*, *eat*, *dress*, and *connect* like the French, part 3 is where the world around you comes into focus. This is where you learn to see beauty everywhere—not because life is perfect but because you've trained your eyes and your mind to catch the poetry in the ordinary.

To the French, true purpose isn't an achievement; it's an ambience. A mood. A way of moving through your day with curiosity and generosity, noticing the details that others rush past. We don't wait for vacations, celebrations, or milestones to feel alive. We create pockets of pleasure in the small things: a well-worn book, a favorite park bench, the smell of something good simmering on the stove.

This section is about those small rituals that give life texture. It's about treating the planet the way we treat friends—with respect, attention, and an understanding that what we nurture nurtures us back. It's about letting art surprise you, reminding yourself that joy doesn't arrive in a package; it appears when you're paying attention.

Before you read on, take a breath. Look around. Whatever room you're in, whatever street you're walking along, there is beauty here—quiet, subtle, waiting. Part 3 will teach you how to find it, how to savor it, and most important, how to let it expand your life from the inside out.

Because when you learn to see the world the French way, even your smallest days become your richest ones.

Chapter 9.

TREAT THE EARTH LIKE A FRIEND

Avec Alex

Growing up, every Sunday morning while the Paris sky was still cloaked in that predawn purple, Maman would rap gently on my door, her voice slipping through like a warm breeze. "Allez, debout, mon cheri, on y va." *Come on, get up, darling, let's go.* I'd roll out of bed, yank on yesterday's jeans—creases and all—skip the mirror entirely, and shuffle down the creaky stairs behind her. Her old wicker basket, weathered and woven tight, swung against her hip with every step like it was keeping time.

The streets of the Seventeenth Arrondissement were ghostly at this hour. A lone taxi might hum by, its headlights cutting through the quiet, or a few pigeons would strut across the cobblestones, owning the place. But that was it—Paris was still rubbing sleep from its eyes. Then we'd turn the corner to Marché Berthier, and whoa, it was like stepping into a different world.

The market was alive, buzzing with energy. Fishmongers heaved crates of ice onto their stalls, the sharp scent of the sea hitting you right in the face. Florists misted their roses and peonies, water droplets catching the first light like tiny prisms. Neighbors leaned over crates of tomatoes, poking and prodding, swapping stories about which ones were juicy enough to eat that very night.

Maman didn't need a shopping list—she navigated the market like a captain steering through familiar waters. First stop was always the mushroom guy. She'd pick up a big, meaty mushroom hold it under my nose, and say, "Breathe it in, *mon ange* (my angel). That's the forest talking." The smell was damp and earthy, like the ground after rain. Next, we'd hit the vegetable stall, where she'd grab a single red radish, rub the dirt off with her thumb, and hand it to me. "Bite," she'd say, and I'd crunch into it, the sharp, peppery snap waking me up better than any coffee. Everything came in brown paper cones or straight from the farmer's hands—no plastic in sight. When it was time to pay, she'd press a few coins into my palm, letting me hand them over, as if I were part of the deal.

The market wasn't just a place to shop—it was our calendar, our connection to the seasons. January meant an abundance of *céleri* (celery) and oysters, the weather so cold they steamed when you cracked them open. Come April, the first *Gariguette* (fresh strawberries) would arrive, nestled in little wooden crates, their sweet perfume screaming spring.

I remember one December, I pointed at a pile of cherries, all glossy and tempting. Maman raised one eyebrow, her signature move, and said, "Pas la saison, mon ange." *Not the season, my angel.* I learned quickly: The earth had its own rhythm, and it wasn't about to bend to a supermarket's schedule.

On the walk home, we'd take our time, her pannier now heavy with treasures. Maman would point out the plane-tree roots buckling the pavement or the stubborn weeds pushing through cracks in the stone. "The city tries to tame nature," she'd say, "but nature always finds a way back." I was usually still half asleep, dragging my feet, but those words stuck with me, like seeds planted deep. Even now, years later, I can't walk past a cracked sidewalk without hearing her voice.

Our kitchen was tiny—six square meters max—but Maman worked it like a Michelin-starred chef. She'd spread the haul across the table: carrots with their feathery tops, leeks still dusted with soil, a wedge of cheese wrapped in wax. Water would be simmering on the stove, a single swirl of olive oil gleaming in the pan. Peels and scraps went into a metal compost tin—almost nothing hit the trash. We ate simply: a bowl of velvety soup, roasted carrots with a sprinkle of thyme, and crusty bread to saucer *le plat*, as she called it, mopping up every last drop. My grandma's old saying rang true: "Do the dishes with your stomach."

Years later, when I was studying in the States, those Sundays haunted me in the best way. I'd walk into a supermarket and see strawberries in October—big, glossy, but smelling like nothing. It felt wrong, like a glitch in the matrix. Trash cans were massive, bigger than the elevator in our old Paris building. I'd watch friends toss half a burger or grab a coffee in yet another disposable cup, and it hit me. They weren't seeing the chain from field to plate to bin.

One day, I caught myself rinsing out a yogurt container, hunting for a yellow recycling bin that didn't exist. My roommates thought I was unhinged, but I couldn't help it—Maman's lessons were hardwired.

I didn't turn into some preachy eco-warrior, though. I just kept my habits close. I bought less, ate everything, and walked anywhere under forty-five minutes—Paris rules, you know? One Saturday, a teammate dragged us an hour out to a farmers' market. Everyone griped about the prices at first, but then we split a peach in the parking lot. The juice ran down our wrists, sticky and sweet, and suddenly nobody cared about the cost. That moment—laughing, licking our fingers—felt like home.

France isn't some green utopia; don't get it twisted. We waste food, too. We take budget flights to Barcelona for a weekend regardless of the emissions. But those Sunday market mornings with Maman taught me some important French cultural touchstones: Buy less, but make it good. Stick to the seasons. Give the peels back to the earth. Use your legs when they'll do the job.

It all started with that radish, Maman's thumb brushing off the dirt, her quiet nudge to pay attention. Even now, when I'm tempted by plastic-wrapped greens or a ten-minute delivery app, I think of her. The planet wasn't some far-off thing. It was right there, walking with us to the market, speaking in the crunch of a radish, the scent of a mushroom, the weight of coins in my hand. When we listened, it gave us what we needed and saved the rest for tomorrow.

GREEN LAWS, SERIOUS BUSINESS

France doesn't play when it comes to the planet, though it hasn't always been this way. Paris air can choke you—pollution levels spike at times, and you can feel the difference in air quality. Industrial farming's still a thing, though organic farms jumped by 30 percent since 2019. But we're moving. Paris's limited driving days, started in 2015, slashed smog by 40 percent. Rewilding efforts are bringing back otters and buzzards. The air quality certificate program Crit'Air has rules that stop high-pollution cars from running on bad air days—drive a clunker, you're out. Single-use plastics? Kicked to the curb in 2020—straws, forks, all of it. Renewables? Solar and wind hit 30 percent of our juice as of a few years ago.

France's got big moves—carbon taxes, urban rewilding, cash for eco-startups—plus grassroots crews planting city forests or scrubbing rivers.

And it's working. A 2022 *Environmental Research Letters* study reported that our green policies slashed emissions by 20 percent since 2005. Between 2005 and 2024, Paris cut nitrogen dioxide and fine particulate matter levels significantly, thanks to bold policies like replacing car lanes with bike paths, eliminating fifty thousand parking spots, and converting busy roads into pedestrian zones.

In our everyday lives, no matter what country we're in, Tom and I push for the same, opting for reusable bags and flatware, and carpooling or walking when it's an option. You can do the same. Let's talk about how to bring eco-conscious living into your life, French style. It's not about being perfect but about showing up, tweaking habits, giving *la terre* (the earth) some love. So start small, feel the rush, and watch your life get *greener.*

THE MARKET IS OUR TURF: HOW TO SHOP FOR GROCERIES

If you want to live a little more à la française, start with your shopping basket. Farmers' markets aren't just charming—they're one of the simplest ways to shrink your footprint while elevating your everyday meals. Unlike supermarket produce shipped across oceans, *marché* goods are grown nearby. That means fewer food miles, fewer trucks on the road, and less carbon in the air. Shopping local can even cut transport emissions significantly. Translation: Your apples don't need a passport to taste amazing.

When you head to a *marché* (or your local equivalent), skip the plastic bags and come armed with canvas totes, baskets, or even an old backpack. Everything's sold loose, so you'll avoid the shrink-wrapped sadness of supermarket veggies and cut down on single-use waste. France has already begun slashing plastics this way—you can, too. Bonus: It feels good to unpack a bag full of real food, not a pile of packaging.

Think seasonally, too. Buy what's ripe right now—strawberries in June, squash in October—rather than relying on hothouse or frozen imports. Not only is it gentler on the planet, but you'll taste the difference immediately. And don't be afraid of the "ugly" produce. Markets thrive on variety, and a wonky carrot or spotted apple is still delicious. In fact, choosing it helps fight food waste.

So here's our challenge for you: This month, swap at least one supermarket trip for a farmers' market visit. Bring your own bags, talk to the growers, taste what's in season, and notice how different it feels. It's not just about shopping—it's about joining a small, delicious rebellion for the planet.

EAT SLOWLY, LIVE BETTER: PRIORITIZE ZERO WASTE

Instead of bulk-buying groceries and letting lettuce turn soggy in the back of the fridge, make daily purchases based on what feels right that day—and actually eat it. For instance, in France we buy just enough bread for that day, no stale ends for the trash.

Speaking of zero waste, France is big on using what you have. It's common for households to make soup from veggie odds and ends. In fact, you can make soup out of nothing but sad carrots, garlic skins, and a leftover thyme branch. Trust us, it will be delicious. There are even restaurants in Paris that pull from nearby farms, and zero-waste chefs who turn potato peels into magic.

Challenge yourself to make a meal out of your leftovers and pantry staples. Pretty much anything can be scrambled with an egg or added to a stir fry. When we cook and eat this way, it is a gesture of respect for the earth that feeds us every day.

PEDAL LIKE MAD MEN: BIKE AND TAKE PUBLIC TRANSIT

Bikes and France? Can't have one without the other. It's in our blood: Tour de France, village bike fests, or just rolling to work with a baguette strapped to your rack. In Paris at any given moment, you'll see people in sharp suits pedaling, briefcases swinging, proving you don't need a Lycra fetish to live it. With 1,400 kilometers of bike lanes and 20,000 Vélib' (rental) bikes, cycling's not a choice—it's a reflex. It's not just Paris either. Bordeaux, Strasbourg, even little La Rochelle are bike crazy, with everyone from all backgrounds pedaling.

Cycling's not just green; it's therapy. Just thirty minutes of biking a day boosts mental health, improves cardio, and cuts heart disease risk by 15 percent. When bike trips in Paris jumped by 70 percent from 2019 to 2023, it made our streets quieter, the air cleaner, and the vibes better. We've ditched car commutes for bike runs, feeling the earth's pulse under our wheels, stress melting like butter in a pan.

Public transportation in France isn't just a convenience—it's part of the culture. You miss a train? No big deal. You glance at the screen; it says "3 minutes," and somewhere a Parisian sighs dramatically as if it's the end of the world. But honestly, that just shows how good the public transportation system is in France. When you think about it, three minutes is a gift. It is just enough time to take a breath, people-watch, or hum along to whatever's playing in your headphones. Trains come so often, you feel like the city's moving with you. If you've lived here, you've probably sprinted for the last *métro*, swapped stories on the platform, or made polite small talk with strangers while secretly watching your bag like a hawk because yes, pickpockets *do* exist and you have to be careful. But at the end of the day, it's all part of the charm.

In fact, the *métro* is where we first learned to read body language, dodge the occasional mysterious puddle, and develop Olympic-level balance during sudden stops. It's also where someone suddenly steps onto the train with an accordion and starts playing loudly—just when you're trying to relax or send a message in peace. You try not to make eye contact, but your foot starts tapping anyway. That's the *métro*: chaotic, human, and somehow always on beat.

France's transit system makes living without a car not just possible but preferable. Whether it's Paris, Lyon, Marseille, or any other major city, public transport shrinks the map. Trains link cities like arteries, trams glide along riverbanks, and most towns are walkable by default. You don't have to "go for a walk"—you're always walking. We don't just move through cities—we absorb them.

And maybe that's the real upside. With every ride, every unexpected detour, you get a little closer to the rhythm of real French life. Sure, sometimes the elevator at your *métro* stop's been broken since 2016. Sure, someone's eating a kebab two inches from your face. But then you glance up, see the Eiffel Tower peeking out beyond the rooftops, and it hits you—you're part of something shared, messy, charming, and very alive.

Even if you don't live in a bike-crazy city, trade one car errand a week for a walk or ride—coffee run, quick grocery trip, whatever's easiest. Treat public transit (or any shared commute) like a pocket of calm: a podcast, a book, a moment to daydream. Explore one new path or neighborhood a month and let inconvenience become ambience. The goal isn't perfection; it's building the reflex to move through your city the French way: slower, lighter, and more aware of the world around you.

THRIFTING FOR THE PLANET: GO FOR SECONDHAND

France loves a good treasure hunt. Secondhand finds—clothes, furniture, odd little objects with stories—are part of the culture. From *vide-greniers* (flea markets) in every village to Parisian *brocantes* (secondhand shops) overflowing with vintage lamps and creaky old chairs, we're out there, digging for gems. Fast fashion's a planet-wrecker—there were seventeen million tons of textile waste in the U.S. alone in 2023—so we stick to durable gear. Buying fewer, better pieces halves waste, but so does shopping secondhand. We thrift or splurge on classics, looking good without killing the earth.

Secondhand apps are huge here, too. The majority of French adults (yep, specifically our parents) use them to sell, buy, or trade everything from sneakers to armoires. It's sustainable, sure, but also social. You never know who you might bond with over a shared love for vintage bikes or antique chairs. Thrifting boosts well-being by fostering community and pride in eco-choices.

If you're on the hunt for something—clothes, décor, furniture, appliances, and so forth—scour your secondhand options first. Check out the marketplaces on social media, your community thrift stores . . . Or for a whole month, challenge yourself to purchase only secondhand. It's not easy or perfect—sorting and searching takes patience—but the thrill of a unique score keeps us hooked. That's the French way: Choose quality, cherish stories, and save the planet one thrift at a time.

THE EARTH'S GIFTS: BRING NATURE TO YOU

Even in big cities like Paris, there are ways to stay connected to nature. We didn't grow up with gardens or fields outside our windows. We grew up in apartments, with courtyards and balconies, but our parents made space for whatever green life they could. My mom grew herbs in yogurt pots—basil, mint, thyme—and knew how to spot wild berries or rosemary sprouting by the sidewalk. She'd bring home chestnuts she found on a walk or dry orange peels for tea. Nothing went to waste. We didn't call it "eco-conscious"—it was just how she lived, and we followed along.

But when we visited our grandparents in the countryside—Tom's in the South near Languedoc-Roussillon—nature wasn't a weekend activity. It was part of everything. The pace slowed. Mornings started with checking the garden. Tomatoes, green beans, plums, figs—we picked what was ripe and planned meals around it. Our grandparents didn't talk about sustainability, but they composted, saved seeds, reused jars, and made everything stretch. The earth gave, and they gave back with quiet consistency.

There was a kind of reverence in the way they lived. Shelling walnuts at the kitchen table. Hanging lavender in bunches to dry. Saving rainwater in big barrels out back. As kids, we didn't see it as special—it was just how things were done. But now we know that was love for the land, passed down by habit, not lecture.

Those summers shaped how we see the world. Even in cities, we carry pieces of that countryside rhythm with us. A pot of basil on the balcony. A trip to the market instead of the supermarket. Noticing what's in season and saying thank you when we eat it.

We're grateful for those quiet lessons—for our parents and grandparents who taught us, without needing to say it out loud, that the earth is a gift. And protecting her isn't a duty—it's a way of showing love in return.

L'histoire de Tom

Everyday Nature

Growing up in a cozy Paris apartment, like so many other Parisians, I learned early on that connecting to the earth doesn't require visiting sprawling fields or rustic farmhouses. Our home was on the eighth floor of a building with no room for an orchard, a vegetable patch, or a chicken coop. But my mom, with her French knack for making the most of what's available, turned our balcony into a pocket of green magic. It was just big enough for a table for four and a few plants. She had five or six little pots brimming with basil, parsley, rosemary, thyme, and sometimes mint. These were her way of bringing the earth into our urban world, a quiet little act of defiance against the concrete jungle outside, and we'd often spend time there, surrounded by her greenery.

Every morning, my mom would step onto the balcony with her coffee, checking on her herbs like they were old friends. She'd water them with care, pinch off dead leaves, and coax them to thrive as long as the Parisian seasons allowed. When she cooked—whether it was a simple omelet or a hearty sauce—she'd slip outside, scissors in hand, and snip a sprig of basil or a few parsley leaves to toss into the pan. The fresh, sharp scent would fill the kitchen, transforming our meals into something alive and rooted.

This wasn't unique to us. Across Paris, balconies and windowsills bloom with herbs, tomatoes, or even strawberries in pots. The balcony gardens aren't just practical. They are a ritual, a way to slow down and stay connected to the rhythms of the earth. Every time we pluck a few pieces for dinner, it feels like honoring that bond, bringing a bit of that Provençal earth to our urban tables.

Funny enough, I've carried this tradition with me. My windowsill, which is much smaller than a balcony, holds a thriving basil plant I'm constantly harvesting from. It's not much—just one plant—but it's the same quiet connection to the earth and everything it offers.

You can grow herbs anywhere—on a fire escape in Brooklyn, a windowsill in London, or a patio in Tokyo. Start with one herb, maybe basil or mint, and let it teach you. Water it, watch it grow, use it in your cooking. It's not about perfection (my basil has had its droopy days) but about presence. You don't need a big budget or a green thumb—just a pot (or even a little cup, really), some soil, and a willingness to try. When life pulls you in a million directions—work, social plans, maybe a family—tending a few herbs is a small but powerful way to slow down. It's a reminder that growth, whether it's a plant or yourself, happens in tiny, consistent steps. And when you toss fresh herbs into your dinner, you'll feel it—a little spark of connection, a taste of the earth beneath the city.

Living well is, at its heart, about loving the planet. And it doesn't have to feel like sacrifice. It can feel like joy, connection, even a playful rebellion against waste. France has shown us that sustainability is woven into the rhythm of everyday life: savoring the story of a tomato in season, pedaling to work with the wind in your hair, honoring the dirt beneath your feet, or giving new life to a thrifted table. When you bring that spirit into your own life, you discover that the green choice is often the richer one. Swap a supermarket run for a farmers' market visit and taste the difference. Carry a tote bag, a water bottle, and a fork in your bag so you're always ready to skip the plastic. Cook what you have instead of letting food languish in the fridge—soup, frittata, and pesto have been making magic from scraps for generations. Walk or bike whenever you can, and you'll notice the world in ways a car window never allows. Choose secondhand before new, and when you do buy new, pick something meant to last. Plant a single herb on a windowsill and use it with reverence. Compost what's left. Adjusting these habits doesn't demand perfection—it asks only for presence and a willingness to care.

What emerges is a way of living that's less about duty and more about delight. Shopping becomes a connection, cooking becomes a gesture of respect, travel becomes a way to see yourself anew. Even the smallest rituals—bringing home produce in paper instead of plastic, or walking a familiar route more slowly—turn into quiet acts of love for the earth.

Green living is not about chasing an image of purity but about showing up, again and again, with intention. When you let the earth into your routines, she rewards you with beauty, health, and perspective. *La vie est plus belle en vert, les amis*—life is more beautiful in green, friends. Now, go live it.

How to Live *Vert* (Green): Our Guide

Hit the Market: Scope out a farmers' market. Grab seasonal stuff—peaches in summer, squash in fall. Chat up vendors, get the dirt on their dirt. No market? Hit grocery stores' local bins or grow basil on your balcony.

Pedal Hard: Bike to work, the bar, or nowhere special. For your next errand, run, walk, or hop on a bus.

Bin the Plastic: Ditch single-use plastics—go for totes, steel bottles, bamboo straws. France's ban proves it works.

Cook Slow, Waste None: Use local, seasonal ingredients. Buy daily or plan tight to skip waste. Turn peels into stock or compost. Hit a farm-to-table spot for dining out. Try cooking with a zero-waste recipe.

Dress Smart, Thrift Smart: Buy quality clothes—jeans that last, a solid jacket. Thrift at markets or on apps for vintage finds. Scope consignment shops before buying new.

Get Dirty: Hike, garden, or picnic in a park. Join a community garden or try foraging.

Fight Green: Back eco-policies—vote, sign petitions, join cleanups. Limiting which cars can drive on which days started with people. Community also drives progress and fuels the work. Start small: Recycle right or join a local green crew.

Toast the Land: Throw a seasonal feast with local goods or hit a harvest fest. Good food, fresh air, your people: perfect combo.

Chapter 10.

SEE ART EVERYWHERE

Avec Alex

If you'd told teenage me that I'd one day be writing about art, I'd have aimed my soccer ball at your shins and cracked up laughing. Art was my dad's obsession, his weekend crusade. While I was itching to escape to the park with my friends, kicking a ball through the dusty streets of our Paris suburb, he'd drag me to galleries, his eyes lit up like a kid's. "Allez, Alex, ouvre les yeux (Come on, Alex, open your eyes)," he'd say, plopping me down on a creaky museum bench in front of a swirling Monet water lily or some stern-faced noble staring out from a gilded frame. "What's this stirring up in you?" I'd roll my eyes, slouch deeper into my hoodie, and mumble, "It's just a painting, Papa." But he'd wait, patient as ever, until I gave in and spilled something—maybe the chaotic blues felt like the knot in my stomach before a big match, or the portrait's glare reminded me of my math teacher's disapproval.

Those talks, sometimes stretching close to an hour, weren't really about the canvas. They were about me untangling my messy teenage thoughts in a quiet space where the world couldn't barge in. I didn't see it then, but those moments were planting seeds, turning art into a lifeline I'd reach for whenever life felt like a storm.

Back then, I thought art was just stuffy museum walls—old paintings for old people. I'd rather have been anywhere else, flirting with girls or joking around with friends at a café. But Dad had this way of making it feel alive. He'd point out the fury in a Delacroix tiger or the loneliness in a Degas dancer's slouch, as if they were telling stories we could both understand.

One Saturday at the Musée d'Orsay, I remember staring at a Van Gogh, all wild stars and swirling skies, and muttering that it looked like how I felt when I couldn't sleep. Dad just nodded, no judgment, and said, "That's what art does, Alex—it holds your chaos so you don't have to." I shrugged it off, but it stuck, like a song you hum without realizing.

Now, as an adult living in the U.S., where life moves at a relentless clip—emails pinging, deadlines looming, traffic snarling—I find myself craving that gallery calm. The States has its own pulse, faster and louder than the cobblestone rhythm of home, and it can leave you dizzy.

My girlfriend, Katherine, is an art fiend. She'd probably pitch a tent in the Louvre's courtyard if they'd let her. She's the one who got me back into galleries, dragging me to local museums or pop-up exhibits in our city. At first, I went along to make her happy, but then I started pulling my dad's old trick. We'd stand in front of a bold, jagged abstract or a soft watercolor that feels like a whisper, and I'd ask, "What's this sparking for you?" It was like free therapy. She'd talk about how a splash of red reminded her of a fight with her boss, or I'd admit a muted gray felt like the weight of a bad week. We'd unravel the stress, the dreams, the what-ifs, all while some painting or sculpture held space for us. It wasn't just about looking. It was about slowing down and finding a rhythm that let us breathe.

Art's not just locked away in museums either. Growing up French, I learned to spot it everywhere. In Paris, it's the graffiti blooming on a concrete wall in Belleville, turning a gray alley into a shout of color. It's the flower fields outside the city, rippling in the wind like one of Monet's fever dreams. It's the old stone buildings in the Marais, their chipped facades carrying centuries of secrets—wars, loves, revolutions—etched into every crack. Even in a city like Chicago, I see it: the murals splashed across warehouse walls, the way the lake catches the sunrise like a canvas, the weathered brick of a dive bar that feels like it's seen a thousand stories. Art's not just something you hang up. It's the world talking to you, if you know how to listen.

Katherine and I have made it a ritual. On tough weeks, we'll hit a gallery or just wander the city, hunting for something that catches our eye—a street artist's stencil, a neon sign flickering in a diner window. It's our way of staying grounded and keeping the chaos at bay. I think back to those museum benches with Dad, how he'd nudge me to name what I felt. He was teaching me that art's a mirror, a way to see yourself more clearly. Now, when life feels like it's spinning too fast, I lean into that lesson. A painting, a mural, even a quiet moment staring at a tree's shadow—it's all a reminder to pause, to feel the world's pulse and your own at the same time.

I've started sharing that with friends here, too. Last month, I dragged my friend Jeff to an exhibit. He's a numbers guy, all spreadsheets and logic, and he walked in skeptical, arms crossed. I pointed to a Rothko, its blurry edges pulsing with color, and asked, "What's this doing to you?" He laughed, said it looked like a sunset on steroids, but then he got quiet.

"Kinda makes me feel small," he admitted, "like the world's bigger than whatever is in my inbox." We stood there for twenty minutes, just talking—about stress, about dreams, about nothing. It felt like those old talks with Dad, like we'd slipped out of time for a bit.

Being French probably wired me for this. We're taught to notice, to let the world's beauty steady us. Here in the U.S., where everything's go-go-go, that habit keeps me curious, less frazzled. Whether I'm in a new city or back in Paris, art's my anchor, a way to find meaning in the mess. It started with Dad, those long museum talks, and now it's mine—a quiet rebellion against the rush, a way to stay open to the world's endless, unspoken stories. This habit can be yours, too.

ART IS THE AIR WE BREATHE

We grew up breathing French art like it's oxygen, not some dusty exhibit behind glass. In France, culture wasn't just a school subject—it was our compass, woven into our streets, our families, our lives. The Louvre is massive, with thirty-five thousand works across three hundred rooms, but it's not just for tourists snapping selfies. On free museum days—the first Sunday of the month, no ticket needed—locals pack in, sketching next to a Delacroix or debating a Cézanne over espresso. The Centre Pompidou, with its colorful pipes and bold modern art, feels like a playground—kids stare wide-eyed at Miró, grandparents ponder Picasso.

But it's not only the big names. Across the country tiny galleries pop up on every corner, run by folks who love art more than money. Provençal villages have their own museums, and city squares hold sculptures you can sit on. A 2025 King's College study found that ten minutes spent with a painting lowers stress and boosts your brain's happy chemicals. That gallery hush we chase? It's like meditation, a break from life's constant chatter.

This openness is pure French. Back in the Renaissance, kings like Francis the First made France an art hub, inviting Leonardo da Vinci to Amboise and filling châteaus with treasures. The French Revolution in 1793 flipped the script—"*art pour tous*" (art for everyone), they said, opening the Louvre to the people, not just nobles. Impressionism in the 1860s—Monet, Renoir, Degas—took it further, painting everyday life like cafés and gardens, not stuffy myths. Today, France spends billions a year on culture, funding street artists, free museum days, and festivals. We grew up with this: School trips to Fontainebleau, sketching gargoyles. Weekends at Normandy galleries where the owner knew our *mamans*. In the U.S., Tom and I hunt that spark—a mural in Canton's arts district, a sculpture in a New Orleans park.

When you think about engaging with art, it's easy to picture grand museums or galleries where people whisper in front of famous paintings. But art isn't just reserved for those spaces. In fact, it's probably already woven into your daily life in ways you might not even notice. A song that lifts your mood, a mural on the side of a building, a handcrafted mug you sip coffee from each morning—these are all forms of art, and they're just as worthy of your attention as the pieces hanging in the Louvre.

The truth is, art is far more approachable, playful, and accessible than we often give it credit for. You don't need to know the "right" terms or carry around an encyclopedia of artists to appreciate it. What you do need is a bit of curiosity and a willingness to pause. When you do, you'll find that art has this quiet magic. It slows you down, shifts your perspective, and invites you to connect—to a place, to a story, or to yourself.

The lesson? Seek art everywhere. Let's explore some of the many ways you can welcome more art into your world. From noticing what's around you to trying your hand at creating something of your own, these are simple, joyful steps anyone can take.

STORIES COME ALIVE

Art may be France's heartbeat, but books are the breath we grew up on. We don't just read; we live with stories. Step into Shakespeare and Company and you'll notice students half asleep over paperbacks while the Seine whispers beyond the window. In my hometown, the *librairie* is still family run. Madame Petit slides the perfect book across the counter and says, "This one's for you."

A 2019 Ministry of Culture survey said 88 percent of French adults read at least one book a year, and nearly a quarter finish more than twenty. Those numbers explain why cafés double as reading rooms: A teenager underlines Camus, a lawyer chuckles at a French *Astérix* comic, a retiree rereads Proust—all at the same zinc bar, no hierarchy, no guilt.

Our romance with words starts *tôt*—early. In primary school, we recite La Fontaine until the lines stick. Later, Molière mocks hypocrisy, Montaigne plants doubt, and Sartre or Beauvoir open the door to existential questions. These texts aren't relics—they're sparring partners for lunch debates.

And the fables come home with us. I still picture an evening in the tiny kitchen of our flat in Alfortville: Papa Bruno is slicing cheese while I brag that I'll "crush" my English project faster than anyone in class. Without even looking up he murmurs, "Souviens-toi du lièvre, mon grand." *Remember the hare, my dear!* Slow down and don't take your superiority for granted. This is of course the message of the fable "The Tortoise and the Hare," in which the slow turtle wins a race against the speedy hare simply because the hare thinks he's got the win so much in the bag that he allows himself to get distracted. I picture the kitchen tiles as a path: Stop bragging, work like the tortoise, and finish.

Another Sunday, a friend drenches me in compliments before asking to borrow my new soccer ball. Papa leans over and whispers, "Attention, le renard." *Beware the fox.* I feel like the gullible crow about to lose its cheese. This is a reference to Jean de la Fontaine's "The Fox and the Crow," another mainstay in French culture. It's a tale that cautions against vanity and falling for flattery. The lesson sticks better than any lecture because it comes as a playful rhyme. Even today, when I open a fable, it feels like looking in a small mirror. The old seventeenth-century words still match what I see in my inbox and newsfeed.

Stories impart important lessons. Some works feel almost civic: *Les Misérables* still teaches compassion, *L'Étranger* makes us look twice at outsiders, and Annie Ernaux proves the personal is political. When Tom and I crave wonder, we reopen *Le Petit Prince*, and the aviator reminds us adulthood can stay curious.

To read here is to fold silences into the day: Observe, reflect, *partager* (share). Under a plane tree in Bordeaux or a maple in Portland, I open a book and the afternoon stretches. Every story lets us live another life, then return to ours with a little more room. Modern research says fiction boosts empathy and calms anxiety—but any French reader could have told you that. Crack a slim paperback on a park bench, and the city drops two *décibels*. The page is a pause button you carry in your pocket.

So, if you wish to live a touch plus français, slip a slim volume into your bag—a book by Zola or Duras, one of the *Tintin* comic series, or a *Dune* novel. *Peu importe*, doesn't matter. Find ten quiet minutes in a café or park or on your front porch. Breathe with the pages. Reflect on one line: What's it saying about you? Then pass the book to a friend. In that small gesture, you'll feel the thread that keeps France stitched together, one shared sentence at a time.

THE MUSIC AND THE STAGE

Music in France is a pulse that pulls you in, makes you move, brings you together. From the soaring violins at the Philharmonie de Paris to a performer's accordion in a park tunnel, it's *partout* (everywhere). Every June 21, the Fête de la Musique turns France into a giant stage—rock bands in Lyon, rappers in Marseille, Breton fiddlers in Quimper, all free, with strangers dancing under streetlights. Music like festival vibes releases oxytocin, bonding people while cutting stress. That's what we feel dancing with strangers, our worries melting away.

Music was our backdrop growing up, even if we didn't realize it then. And we still chase that joy—stopping for a guitarist in a park, hitting festivals, or DJing our own tracks. We don't need to read proof that music boosts serotonin, lifting your mood in minutes—we've felt it. And we know you have, too. That feeling of driving with the window down when your jam comes on? Nothing better. More of that, we say.

So, chase music. Stop for a street performer or hit a local gig—bar band, choir, open mic. Dance if it moves you. Make a playlist of songs that hit your heart and share it. Host a music night—everyone brings a song, like the Fête de la Musique at home.

L'histoire de Tom

Spectacular Art in Everyday Places

When my to-do list towers and I feel overwhelmed, I seek out art to reset. It doesn't have to be a museum, though I love those. Here in New Orleans where I live, art is everywhere, woven into the city's soul. Sculpture gardens spill over with bold forms, botanical gardens burst with color, and historic homes flaunt details that stop you in your tracks.

One of my favorite places in the entire city is the Sydney and Walda Besthoff Sculpture Garden inside City Park. It's hands down my favorite sculpture garden in the world. Every time a friend or family member comes to visit, I take them there. I never get tired of it—it's so peaceful, open, and full of surprises. There's always something new to notice.

New Orleans makes it easy to find art in unexpected places. Houses alone are worth slowing down for. There's this one house in my neighborhood that goes all out, decorating for every season like it's a Broadway production. Christmas lights in December, spooky skeletons for Halloween, pastel bunnies for Easter—every month, it's a new spectacle. I make a point to jog by, grinning at their fearless creativity.

What I love most about art is the freedom it gives you to decide what it means. I like to stand in front of a painting or sculpture, letting my mind weave a story—maybe a splash of red is anger, or a twisted bronze figure is chasing a dream. Then I'll read the plaque or dig online, only to find I'm either spot-on or wildly off, discovering it's about something completely different, like a farmers' market or a forgotten war. There's no wrong or right answer, just the joy of wondering.

Art elevates any space it touches. It's paintings and statues, yes, but it's also the rhythm of a jazz tune, the alchemy of a well-cooked meal, the way fairy lights drape tree branches at night, turning an ordinary street into magic.

I dabble in art myself, sketching abstract doodles—blobs of color, jagged shapes, nothing polished but entirely mine. My apartment has a few of these pieces on the walls, not because they're gallery-worthy but because they're my own. They help me make sense of things. Art is like that. It's not about perfection. It's a language you can speak even if you're not fluent. You just have to pause long enough to listen.

THE CINEMA

France invented *le cinéma*—shout-out to the Lumière brothers in 1895—and we've been obsessed ever since. Movies aren't just entertainment; they're conversations. Historic theaters like Le Grand Rex, with its art deco glow, feel like stepping into a dream. Small-town cinema clubs pack in locals debating documentaries or classics like *Les Parapluies de Cherbourg.* The Cannes Film Festival, born in 1946, is a global stage—glam, sure, but also a place for ideas, where people marvel and argue over films. Moviegoing sharpens your brain and lifts your mood, thanks to the stories and shared enthusiasm.

Amélie in particular is a French touchstone. Its Montmartre, with cobblestone streets and quirky cafés, feels like the Paris we know—timeless, alive, full of small joys like cracking crème brûlée or skipping stones on the Canal Saint-Martin. It's a love letter to the French *art de vivre*, finding magic in the everyday. It's charming and everything we love about our culture. *Amélie*'s spark—its call to savor life's details—reminds the viewer to stay grounded, notice the poetry in a grocer's smile or a city's hum. It's everything films should bring to our lives.

We recommend you dive into cinema. Watch the classics. Note one feeling a film sparks. Discuss it with a friend or join a film club (community centers often have them). Re-create the French ritual: dim lights, no phones, savor the story.

HERITAGE LIVES

France is a living museum—Paris's medieval Marais, Haussmann's grand boulevards, the Louvre's glass pyramid blending centuries. Versailles hosts concerts in its gilded halls. Provençal villages throw lavender festivals with folk dances. Brittany's Celtic nights, with bagpipes and storytelling, keep myths alive. Appreciating heritage boosts pride, curiosity, and wellbeing. It doesn't have to be a grand excursion either. Local landmarks, Native American museums, and historical graveyards feel rooted yet open to the now.

France balances old and new like a pro. Post-Revolution, "liberté, égalité, fraternité" (freedom, equality, brotherhood) made culture public—museums, theaters, and libraries for all. Today, France funds artists with millions in grants yearly, from street muralists to composers. Regional heritage shines, like Alsace's Christmas markets, Corsica's polyphonic choirs, and Normandy's cider festivals. Joining others in local traditions cuts loneliness by fostering belonging. We feel this—art in the everyday, keeping us tethered to our roots.

Try mixing old and new into your life, too. Learn about your town's history. Visit a historic site, like an old church or a museum. Learn its story online so you can really understand its origins. Then hit a modern exhibit, street fair, or new mural. Pause and reflect on what you've learned. Ask yourself, "What did I learn? How do I feel?" Write it out in your journal or a note on your phone, or tell a friend.

Art pulls us out of our heads, into the moment, and into each other. It's why we stop when we hear a talented musician on the street, rewatch our favorite films, or doodle on a whim. In a world that can at times feel so lonely, our tendency as creatures to congregate together around a shared love of a particular art form heals. So make art social. Drag friends to a museum, book fair, or concert. Host a movie night or potluck with a cultural theme (French cheese, anyone?). Shared culture strengthens bonds.

But above all, create freely. Paint, write, strum, cook—it doesn't need to be good. Try a doodle, a haiku, or a knitting project. Expression lifts self-esteem. Our bad sketches? They're ours, and they feel great. Check community centers for art classes or YouTube for tutorials. If you've got time for Netflix, you've got fifteen minutes for art.

Remember, art's about feeling, not skill—nobody's judging your drawing or playlist. No galleries nearby? Find the art in your town's architecture, street signs, and local park. Art is everywhere. Accessing it is about showing up curious, ready to feel alive. Even small cultural acts boost belonging, so take the leap.

Chapter 11.

FIND JOY IN RITUAL

Avec Tom

One of the rituals that keeps me anchored more than anything else is my daily call with my brother, Sam. There's nothing orchestrated about it, nothing grand. It's simply something that settled into my life the way good habits do: naturally, quietly, almost without asking permission.

Every evening, usually right before I head to the gym, I call him. Or he calls me. It doesn't matter who starts it; it's part of the rhythm of our days now, like a soft punctuation mark between afternoon and evening.

Sam lives in Texas, finishing his master's degree, and even though we're in different states, the distance hasn't touched our closeness. If anything, we've grown even more connected. We've always been like that: same passions, same hobbies, same borderline obsessive love for soccer, same appreciation for a good meal. Talking is easy. Being ourselves is easy.

Growing up, we were inseparable. And now that we both live in the U.S., it still feels like we're just down the hall from each other. Our calls are rarely about anything remarkable, which is precisely what makes them matter. Some days we spend an hour dissecting a match we watched. Other days we talk about what we're cooking for dinner. And sometimes (my favorite times) we just stay on the line in companionable silence, each doing our own thing, not feeling the need to perform or fill space.

There's a comfort in that kind of connection, the kind you share only with someone who knows you deeply and has known you always. These video calls have become our way of seeing each other every day without actually being in the same room. They keep us updated, yes, but more important, they keep the relationship alive in the simplest, most unforced way.

We give each other advice, complain about life, plan trips, send each other memes, laugh at things that make sense only to us. The call is a reminder that even when everything around us shifts and changes, this—this bond, this touchpoint—doesn't. It feels like home.

For someone else, it might be just a phone call. But for me, it's a ritual. A small, loyal thread that keeps life feeling connected. And maybe that's what happiness often looks like: something simple, steady, and shared with someone you love.

Without this call, I'd feel like my day wasn't complete. There's something about that connection to my brother that grounds me and gives me a feeling of being whole.

The French way is full of ritual. Whether we're meeting for a game of soccer in the park, where strangers cheer and friends roast your bad passes, or greeting someone with a kiss on the cheek instead of a wave, or picking up a warm pastry in the morning, these small, consistent rituals create meaning. In a world of deadlines and lonely screens, these constant cultural practices are also our secret sauce for happiness. They are what keep life *sympa* (nice). They reduce stress, invite joy, and most important, bring people together. They turn ordinary moments into something magical, reminding us of who we are, where we come from, and what really matters.

That's the power of the little things that stitch our daily life together. They don't demand much, but they give you everything. A bit of structure, a sense of belonging, and a daily sense of comfort.

Alex and I have developed our own rituals, mixing how we were raised with the rhythm of our current lives. We're all about trying to be as efficient and professional as possible in our day-to-day, but we still leave space for fun, health (mental and physical), and friendship. We work hard, but we also enjoy hard. Because if you're not laughing, sharing, or just taking the time to sit down with people who matter, what is the point?

So, whatever your "phone call moment" is, hold on to it. Or even better, start one today. In this chapter, we'll show you our favorite French rituals you can riff on, many of which might already be familiar to you.

But first, a word about what makes rituals so powerful.

THE GIFTS OF RITUALS

A ritual is something you do almost without thinking but would notice right away if it went missing. It's personal and can be rooted in how you were raised, where you come from, and what you care about. It's the reason life still feels human when everything else feels chaotic.

But rituals are more than cute habits. They regulate your nervous system. They create emotional predictability in a chaotic world. They add meaning to the mundane. They give your brain something to return to when everything feels overwhelming. Most important, rituals create micro-moments of joy you can count on. With ritual, joy stops being accidental. It becomes accessible.

If you're still skeptical, here's some science for you: A 2019 *British Journal of Psychiatry* study found that cultural traditions cut depression risk by 30 percent, giving structure when life's a mess. *L'apéro* with friends, Sunday lunches, festival dances—they pull us together, fighting the loneliness that hits 25 percent of young adults (Gallup study from 2023). Communal rituals help create a sense of belonging, acting like glue for scattered lives. We've felt it: clinking glasses in a friend's courtyard, our worries fading, or letting loose at a concert, strangers becoming friends. It's often the little routines, like a morning coffee or an evening walk, that help us stay present, anchor us in the moment, and lift our happiness daily.

It's for these reasons we keep certain traditions—hosting potlucks, joining local groups. Because rituals aren't just French; they're human.

But speaking of French rituals, here are a few of our favorites you can borrow, ranging from the daily to the weekly and seasonal.

THE BED IS THE STARTING POINT

In France, making the bed isn't a chore squeezed between toothpaste and the school run. We see it as a *ritual*—quiet, quick, almost ceremonial. While other cultures sometimes treat the bed like a soft-fabric filing cabinet (pajamas here, last night's hoodie there, maybe the dog somewhere under the duvet), the French approach it with a touch of reverence. Not preciousness so much as *presence.*

We like to think of it as *How do I want my day to feel when I come back to this room?*

Each morning, linens are smoothed, pillows fluffed, the duvet shaken out like a fresh breath. Not military corners, just an intentional reset. It's less about perfection and more about a promise to yourself: You will end your day in a space that feels calm, not chaotic.

And because it's done daily, there's no mountain of laundry to fight later, no tangled sheets waiting to ambush you at bedtime, no bedroom that looks like the aftermath of a particularly passionate nap. It's a ritual that eliminates the slow creep of clutter. No crumpled blankets lurking like regrets. No piles of stuff migrating from one surface to another. Just clarity.

The beauty is in the smallness of it. Two minutes, sometimes three, never more.

A tiny act that tells your brain, *The day is underway. The night will return. And you, dear human, are holding the thread between them.*

Each gesture becomes its own ceremony: folding back the edges, opening the shutters to let light spill over newly smoothed sheets, placing a book back on the nightstand with intention instead of chaos. These tiny actions anchor you. They make the room feel like a refuge instead of a staging area. And because the bed is made, the whole home feels subtly more held together. You move differently. You breathe differently. You return at the end of the day to a space that feels welcoming, not demanding.

Look, we're not saying making the bed is anything

groundbreaking—and we're certainly not suggesting that people elsewhere don't do it. Of course they do. It's simply that in France it carries a little extra weight. It's part of the rhythm, the ritual, the quiet choreography of the morning. One small act that signals intention, beauty, and care before the rest of the day comes rushing in.

LETTING THE DAY IN

For the French, the morning doesn't officially begin until you open the windows. It's as essential as coffee, as instinctive as breathing. Even in the dead of winter, even if it means a brief gust of cold air slapping you awake, the French push open the shutters or windows and let the outside in. We're not going for ventilation as much as renewal. It's a quiet, domestic reset that welcomes the day into our homes.

For a few minutes, the home breathes with the world. Night air drifts out, morning air sighs in. The curtains lift. Sounds from the street rise up—a scooter, a bakery truck, a neighbor's radio, a child laughing on the sidewalk. Life reenters the home gently, naturally, before screens or schedules or noise intrude.

And because this happens *every* morning, the ritual keeps the home feeling lighter, fresher, almost spiritually decluttered. No stuffy rooms. No sleep lingering in corners. No home that feels "closed." Instead, there's movement: air, light, scent, season, all flowing through, reminding you that your space is alive.

This tiny act also keeps things healthier without much thought. Fewer odors. Less humidity. A reset of energy. It's invisible maintenance wrapped inside a moment of mindfulness.

Each gesture becomes its own ceremony: the click of the latch, the sweep of the shutters, the first breath of cool morning air across your face. You feel the weather, the temperature, the mood of the city. You get information no app can give you. And because it takes less than a minute, it becomes a small touchstone of consistency, a moment that belongs to you, no matter how chaotic the rest of the day becomes.

This breezy ritual is a way of saying, *The day is new. Let's begin it together.*

THE DAILY SHOP

In France, grocery shopping is often a daily ritual, not a weekly requirement. It's a *rituel.* A gentle, grounding loop that quietly structures the day. While Americans rally for their "big shop" like they're prepping for a snowstorm with giant carts, giant lists, and giant jars of pickles, the French slip out with a small tote and a sense of curiosity.

The question isn't "What do I need for the week?" It's *"What feels right today?"*

The daily shop is less about provisioning and more about presence. You stop by the bakery for bread that's still warm, exchange a quick hello with the *boulangère* (baker), then wander to the produce stand to see what looks beautiful. Not perfect but *beautiful*. Maybe the tomatoes smell incredible today. Maybe the strawberries came in early. Maybe the radishes look smug and irresistible.

And because you're shopping this way, little by little and day by day you always end up with the freshest of everything. No forgotten broccoli dissolving into mush in the chill drawer. No fridge so overstuffed it feels like a storage unit. Daily shopping naturally means less waste, fewer regrets, and more intentional eating. You buy what you love, and you eat what you buy!

Since you're buying only what you'll eat today or tomorrow, there's no pressure, no overthinking, no meal-planning matrix. You choose ingredients the way you choose moods: Light. Simple. Fresh. Inspiration first, logistics second.

The ritual works because it's small. Manageable. Human. It breaks up your day, inviting you into the smells, into the season. It punctuates the morning or the late afternoon, a soft transition between "before" and "after." So instead of looking at grocery shopping as a chore to finish, try approaching it like the French by seeing it as a way to feel fulfilled, connected, and quietly luxurious.

APÉRO, IT'S SACRED

If France has a religion, *l'apéro* is its daily mass. It's that golden hour before dinner full of drinks, nibbles, and socializing, when the day's stress melts like butter in a pan. We pile into our mate's courtyard, clinking glasses, passing olives and crusty bread while swapping stories from our lives. No phones, just chatter, laughs, and good times. *L'apéro*'s not just a drink—it's a ritual that says, "Slow down, connect." Shared meals or drinks boost oxytocin, bonding you to the people you're spending time with. Now, living abroad, Alex and I keep it going, whether it's meeting up with friends for happy hour or hosting *apéro* with whatever's handy—chips and guac, ordering tacos, whatever works. Having these social rituals makes every day feel like a mini-festival of life.

CELEBRATION IS LIFE

France's calendar is a party that never stops. Bastille Day, July 14, lights up the sky: fireworks over the Seine, parades in every town, kids waving flags and sneaking extra *bonbons* (candies). The Fête de la Musique, on June 21, turns streets into stages—rockers in Marseille, fiddlers in Brittany, many enjoying beers and dancing badly to a Lyon jazz band. These events are France's pulse, blending history with pure joy. These celebrations have a way of making everyone feel like they belong, like they are a part of a tribe, even if they're rolling solo.

On the other side of this, a French person wandering through a Fourth of July parade or a county fair might be floored by the Americana of it all—as we were initially. The patriotism of it all, not to mention the corn dogs and kettle corn, the kids sticky with popsicles, the neighbors throwing blankets down on the grass for fireworks. These celebratory moments, big or small, are worth savoring. Do it more often! Don't skip the fair just because it feels corny, or stay home because you're tired—show up, soak it in, and let yourself belong to the crowd for a night.

And if your calendar feels bare, invent your own *fêtes*. Celebrate the first day of summer with a picnic in the park. Mark the autumnal equinox with a bonfire and s'mores. Have friends over every year on the longest night of winter to cook something cozy and raise a glass. France reminds us that rituals—whether official holidays or ones we make up ourselves—are less about perfection and more about connection. The trick is simply to gather, to mark the moment, and to give joy and connection a place to live.

REGIONS, OUR ROOTS

France's rituals are as varied as its landscapes. Provence boasts beautiful lavender fests. Brittany's maritime festivals honor the sea with oyster feasts and bagpipe wails. Alsace's Christmas markets glow with mulled wine and gingerbread, families skating under twinkling lights.

We grew up with this diversity: Normandy's cider fests, Corsica's chestnut fairs, Lyon's silk-weaving celebrations. Each region's rituals felt like ours, whether we were slurping oysters or dancing in a Provençal square. Abroad, we do our best to seek it out through state fairs and cultural events, chasing that French spark where local pride meets shared joy.

We were quick to observe how much multicultural richness already exists outside of France, especially in places like the U.S. where dozens of cultures live side by side. Oktoberfest in Cincinnati, Lunar New Year parades in San Francisco, Juneteenth block parties in Texas, Puerto Rican Day in New York—these are not "someone else's" celebrations; they're invitations to step into the heartbeat of a community.

The French know that connection is something anyone, anywhere, can practice. So the next time your town hosts a Greek festival, a Diwali celebration, or a powwow, don't just read about it—go. Taste the food, listen to the music, let yourself be pulled into a tradition filled with rituals that may not be your own but can still shape your sense of place. France taught us that rituals are roots, and when you participate, even as an outsider, you get to borrow that sense of belonging for yourself.

L'histoire d'Alex

Find Your Lake Moment

For a long time, I didn't realize how much I needed ritual until I went through a period where every day felt unstructured and a little hollow. Nothing was "wrong," per se, but nothing felt rooted either. It was a really busy time at work . . . I kept searching for big happiness when what I actually needed was rhythm, something tiny and steady to hold on to. It wasn't until my girlfriend and I began our own small ritual that I found the balance I craved.

There's this lake near my home in California, which funny enough inspired a French painting with its glassy water and soft, painterly light. It became my girlfriend Kat's and my *endroit sacré*, our sacred spot, especially early in the morning when the world's still quiet and it's just us, the water, and the whispering trees. No crowds, just perfect California weather—crisp and golden, like a postcard you want to live in. For five years now, we've made walking around this lake our morning ritual, and let me tell you, it's the sweetest way to start the day, with connection and intention.

Here's our rule: no phones. I leave mine in the car, and she does, too. No scrolling, no notifications, just us, talking, really talking. We stroll for fifteen to twenty minutes—sometimes two laps if we've got time before a meeting—pouring out whatever's on our minds. What's stressing us? What's got us excited? How can we make today better for each other? It's like our own soulful chat where we share anxieties, dreams, or just laugh about nothing. Sometimes we grab a coffee and sip it as we wander, the lake reflecting the sky like a Monet canvas, setting the mood for something deep and real.

This ritual, it's not always picture-perfect. Some mornings, we're in sync, waking up happy, buzzing about a day full of promise. Other times, we start with a disagreement—maybe I'm grumpy about work or she's stressed about a deadline. But that's life, yeah? The lake doesn't judge; it just listens as we work it out, step-by-step. Over five years, we've seen our talks evolve, like the seasons. Back when we were in college, it was all about exams, parties, dreams of "someday." Now, with Kat finishing her master's, we're dreaming bigger—talking about the future, where we'll live, our take on kids. At 7 a.m., no less! But those early chats, they set the tone. They're the perfect way to start the morning.

What I especially love is how this ritual grounds us. No phones means no distractions, just us, present. I remember that she is my priority, and I hope I'm hers. We end our day with Pilates together, but the lake is where it begins, where we choose each other before the world rushes in. It puts me in this content mood—happy, clear-headed, ready to tackle the day. Communication is the heartbeat of a couple. And starting with these walks, it's like we're saying, "You come first."

My advice: Find your lake, your ritual, leave the phone behind, and start your day with what matters most. That's love, that's French.

BUILD YOUR OWN RITUAL

Ritual looks different wherever you are: tailgates, Sunday trips to Trader Joe's, stopping at the same place every time you take a long drive. There's joy in those rituals, too. The point isn't to adopt French rituals exactly. It's to notice which rituals in any culture bring you back to yourself.

The French don't let busy lives kill their rituals—they adapt. In Paris, where schedules are wild, *apéro* might be a quick rosé, not a three-hour saga. Families squeeze in week-day dinners, thirty minutes of *blanquette de veau* (veal dish) and banter. Virtual toasts over Zoom kept us sane during lockdowns, clinking screens with cousins near and far. When rituals are flexible, they make it easier to stay close, even on a tight schedule.

HOW TO BUILD A RITUAL (THE FRENCHIE WAY)

You don't need lavender fields or Parisian balconies to be as ritual-centric as the French. You just need intention. Rituals—whether daily, weekly, or seasonal—are less about perfection and more about rhythm. They're the gentle touchpoints that make life feel a little steadier, a little softer, a little more *yours*.

1. Start with a craving, not a chore.

Identify an area in your life where you'd like more ease, structure, or comfort. If you want to feel more productive, create a morning ritual of making a quick to-do list before opening your inbox. Or if, like Alex, you want to feel more grounded, step outside first thing in the morning and go for an invigorating walk. If stress is messing with your evenings, claim an hour to read, paint, wander, or do whatever makes you feel at peace.

2. Choose something small, doable, and accessible.

Rituals don't have to be grand. They can be as basic as one deep breath, a five-minute walk, or lighting a candle before opening your laptop. If it feels manageable on your hardest day, it will stick.

3. Let the ritual connect you.

In case you haven't noticed, most of our rituals are rooted in connection—to nature, others, or yourself. The best rituals open a window. Can it be done outdoors? Can it include light, air, water, plants? Can someone join you—your partner, friend, a neighbor? Rituals are most powerful when they root you to something larger.

4. Be consistent, but keep it gentle.

Rituals thrive on rhythm, not rigidity. You want repetition, not the pressure to be perfect. It should feel like a gift you give yourself, not a performance you owe to anyone else. A few tips to help rituals stick:

1. Pair it with something you already do.
   i. Brush teeth + gratitude list
   ii. Morning coffee + journaling
   iii. Driving to work + listen to a playlist that gives good vibes

2. Make it proximity friendly.
   i. Place your journal next to your coffee machine.
   ii. Keep a pair of sneakers in the car so you can go for a walk at any time.

3. Be extra about it.
   i. Buy shoes you love to walk in.
   ii. Splurge for the nicer sheets.
   iii. Give your next potluck a theme.

Follow our ways to weave French-inspired rituals into your life, sparking joy and connection, *tranquille* (relax)-style. Start small and, more important, make it yours.

Host an Apéro: Grab friends, drinks (wine, soda, whatever), and nibbles—chips, cheese, olives. Set a table, chat for an hour, no phones. Studies have shown that shared tables bond people.

Celebrate the Season: Join a local festival—music, food, culture—or host your own. Think Bastille Day vibes: grill, play tunes, invite neighbors. Check online for events or start your own.

Savor Morning Moments: Take your time at a café, park bench, or window. Take ten minutes to unplug. Watch the world, like our bistro mornings back home.

Take Evening Strolls: Walk after dinner—park, street, anywhere—and don't rush. We know firsthand that walking cuts stress.

Gather at the Table: Host a family or friend dinner—simple stuff, like pasta or market veggies. Linger, talk, laugh. Make it a ritual, monthly, or weekly if you're keen. Small table? Potluck it.

Make It Yours: Create a personal ritual: weekly movie night, journaling, gardening. Tie it to joy. An easy one we get into? Create a Sunday playlist, and listen to it weekly.

In the end, finding joy in the rituals is about remembering who you were before life became so busy. The child who loved routines. The teenager who found comfort in small consistency. The adult who still pauses every now and then when something beautiful interrupts the noise.

Joy isn't a lightning bolt. It's a rhythm. A practice. A ritual.

And when you answer it, when you honor the tiny, steady, beautifully human rituals woven into your day—you realize you're not just surviving your life. You're living it.

One small ritual at a time.

IN CONCLUSION:
Make Every Day More French

We didn't set out to write a manifesto. We were just two French kids chasing something across the Atlantic—maybe a future, maybe a feeling. What we found instead was a bridge between worlds. Somewhere between a Burgundy parking lot and a Charleston beach, we learned this truth: The French way of life—our way—has something real to offer. Not because it's flawless but because it's intentional. Present. Alive.

About five years after we started AT Frenchies in Charleston, a man approached us at the Coachella music and arts festival to say thanks. He had struggled with mental health during the pandemic and found strength in our content and humor. We knew we were entertaining and educating people on French language and culture, but this moment made us realize how French lifestyle and attitudes could genuinely help people reframe their thinking and live better lives.

While he was the first, he is not the only one who has either walked up to us or reached out to us online to express similar feelings. Honestly, we take this as the most sincere form of appreciation for what we do. They are at the core of why we decided to pursue writing this book.

This book isn't about telling you how to live—it's about showing you how we live and how it's helped us find joy even in messiness, so maybe it can help you now, too. And now, as we say *au revoir* (for now), we want to leave you with something more than stories. We want to give you a starting point. A way to bring the best of France into your daily life, no matter your ZIP code.

Because the French mindset is about *how* you do what you do. It's about choosing presence over performance, meaning over metrics, and quality over quantity—in food, in relationships, in how you spend your one wild life.

So here are the highlights: a simple guide to living more à la française—not in Paris but right where you are.

Live Slower. Savor Longer. Pause when you pour your coffee. Sit when you eat. Taste your food. Listen—really listen—when someone's talking. Take the long way. Stretch the moment. You don't need a long lunch break, just a long *breath* in between tasks.

Edit Your Life Like a French Closet. French people don't have more—they have better. Choose fewer things, but let them matter more. Your wardrobe. Your schedule. Your relationships. Curate your life like it's your favorite playlist. Keep what brings joy. Let go of what doesn't fit anymore.

Make Meals Ritual, Not Routine. A proper meal isn't about the food—it's about what happens around it. Set the table. Light a candle on a Tuesday. Invite someone over. Even takeout tastes different when eaten with real plates and intention.

Say No—Graciously, Often. The French are masters of the gentle no. They protect their time, their peace, and their boundaries. You can, too. Say no to hustle culture. Say no to plans you don't want. Say no so you can say *yes* to what actually matters.

Choose Curiosity over Control. Not everything needs to be optimized. Let some things be messy. Try things just for the joy of trying. Ask questions. Take detours. Let yourself *wonder* instead of always needing to *win*.

Love Big, but Keep It Classy. Affection doesn't need to be loud to be real. Hold hands. Make eye contact. Write love notes. Pick connection over performance—because the best kind of romance is the one that doesn't need a post to prove it.

Find Art Everywhere. You don't need a gallery to see beauty. It's in the way an espresso steams. The crack in the sidewalk. The laugh of your best friend. The smell of the bakery down the block. *That* is *art de vivre*—seeing the poetry in the ordinary.

We're not telling you to become French. We're saying

take what works. Let the good stuff cross borders. These little habits—lingering, listening, noticing—don't require a passport. They just require presence.

So here's your invitation. Pick one small ritual. Make it yours. Then another. Then another. Let your life get a little softer, a little slower, a little more sparkly around the edges. That's what this book has always been about. Not chasing the French dream but weaving parts of it into the life you already have. A life with more taste, more tenderness, and more truth.

And if you need us? We'll be out there, too—still dreaming, still dropping cheese crumbs on our shirts, still laughing too loud at *apéro*. Rooting for you. Always.

Vive la vie, mes amis. Go live it well.

Alex and Tom

Acknowledgments

To our families: Tom's parents, Virginie and Noël, and Alex's parents, Sandra and Bruno; thank you for being the steady backdrop to everything we do. For the encouragement that was loud when we needed it and quiet when we didn't. For the patience, the perspective, and the unwavering belief that following your instincts is always worth the risk.

To our siblings: Alex's sister, Clara, and Tom's brother, Sam; thank you for being our built-in best friends, our reality checks, and our safe place. For the daily calls, the constant support, and the unconditional love that keeps us grounded no matter where life takes us.

To Mattie and Kat, thank you for loving us through the writing of this book and all the versions of us that came with it. For your patience, your honesty, your encouragement, and for reminding us to breathe, laugh, and stay present when things felt overwhelming. This book carries so much of your support within it.

And to our friends, confidants, and chosen family, thank

you for being part of the rhythm of our lives. For the check-ins, the late nights, the honest feedback, the laughter, and the reminders of who we are outside work. All of it matters more than you know.

To our agents, Steve Troha, Sophie Brett-Chin, and Beth Rosenthal, thank you for believing in this project from day one and guiding us through every step with clarity, patience, and encouragement.

To our editors at Penguin Random House, Nina Rodriguez-Marty and Jenn Houghton, thank you for your thoughtful guidance, your trust, and for helping shape this book into what it was meant to be.

To Penguin Random House, thank you for giving this project a home and for believing in our voices so wholeheartedly. We are deeply grateful to our extraordinary team—Dave Litman, Logan Hill, Naomi Burns, Julia Falkner, Rachel Wainz, Meg Leder, and Brian Tart—for their talent, care, and dedication in bringing this book to life. It's been an honor to collaborate with this team, and we sincerely thank you!

To our collaborator, Allie Kingsley Baker, thank you for your creativity and insight, and for helping bring our ideas to life in such meaningful ways.

To our illustrator, Amy Jindra Hodgson, thank you for translating emotion into images and for giving this book its visual soul.

Glossary of French Terms

apéro (**masc.**) ***(ah-peh-ro)***

Short for *apéritif.* The sacred French ritual of predinner drinks and nibbles—equal parts unwind and connect.

art de vivre (**masc.**) ***(ar duh veev-ruh)***

The "art of living." A philosophy of savoring life slowly, beautifully, and on purpose.

au revoir ***(oh ruh-vwar)***

"Until we see each other again." The elegant French goodbye.

bienvenue ***(bee-ehn-veh-new)***

Welcome! Often said with warmth, a cheek kiss, and maybe a glass of wine.

bon appétit ***(bon ah-peh-tee)***

Enjoy your meal. Said before eating—it's more than polite; it's sacred.

c'est la vie ***(say lah vee)***

"That's life." A verbal shrug used when things don't go to plan (and they rarely do).

chic ***(sheek)***

Stylish, elegant, timeless. Applies to outfits, interiors, table settings, and attitudes.

Comté (**masc.**) ***(kohm-tay)***

A beloved semihard French cheese with a nutty flavor—best served with a crusty baguette and zero guilt.

digestif (**masc.**) ***(dee-zheh-steef)***

An after-dinner drink meant to help digestion (and extend conversation). Think cognac, armagnac, or herbal liqueurs.

entrée (**fem.**) ***(on-tray)***

The first course—not the main dish. Usually light and lovely: a soup, salad, or savory tart.

fin (**fem.**) ***(fahN)***

The end. Of the meal, the night, or the story. Often marked with espresso.

fromage (**masc.**) ***(fro-mazh)***

Cheese. Deeply revered, often consumed, never rushed.

marché (masc.) ***(mar-shay)***

Market.

merci *(mehr-see)*

Thank you. Always sincere, often repeated.

non *(nohN)*

No. Frequently used. Occasionally softened with a smile.

oui *(wee)*

Yes. Usually followed by wine or a better question.

petit (masc.) ***(puh-tee)* / petite** (fem.) ***(puh-teet)***

Little or small. Used affectionately—*une petite robe* (a cute little dress), *un petit café* (a quick espresso).

plat principal (masc.) ***(plah prahn-see-pal)***

The main course. The star of the show, often served solo for full appreciation.

très bien *(tray byehN)*

Very good. A French stamp of approval on food, style, or a well-told story.